Get It Right
Your Choice
Is Your Destiny

Get It Right
Your Choice
Is Your Destiny

Emmanuel Goshen

Published by Edson Consultancy, 2021

© Copyright Edson Consultancy 2021

GET IT RIGHT
YOUR CHOICE IS YOUR DESTINY

All rights reserved.
The right of Emmanuel Goshen to be identified as the author of this work has been asserted in accordance with the Copyright, Designs and Patents Act 1988.

No part of this publication may be reproduced, stored in a retrieval system, or transmitted, in any form or by any means, electronic, mechanical, photocopying, recording or otherwise, nor translated into a machine language, without the written permission of the publisher.

This is a work of fiction. Names, characters, places and incidents are the product of the author's imagination or are used fictitiously. Any resemblance to actual persons, living or dead, events or locales is entirely coincidental.

Condition of sale. This book is sold subject to the condition that it shall not, by way of trade or otherwise, be lent, re-sold, hired out or otherwise circulated in any form of binding or cover other than that in which it is published and without a similar condition including this condition being imposed on the subsequent purchaser.

ISBN 978-0-995-74686-2

Contents

Your Choice Either Make Or Break You 1
The Power Of Your Choice 10
Why make choices? 17
Drive Your World 23
Set Peak Standards 32
Choose To Be Enlighten 40
Be Bold And Face Your Fears 50
Live In The Present 56
Stand For Something Or Fall For Anything 62
Getting Rid Of Negative Voices 70
Stay Connected To Your Goals 75
Learn From All Mistakes 81
Keep Moving Forward 88
Three Vital Nuggets 94
Take This Home 102

Other Books By Emmanuel Goshen

The leader's supplement: A major Platform for High Performance Leadership

The 7 Laws of Productivity: Make Your Vision a Reality

The 7 Principles of Transformation: Accomplishing your goals with the Right Insight

The Mysteries of Excellence: Graduating from Challenges to a Champion Arena

Integrity: An Act of Distinction

Dedication

The success of this book is dedicated to the Almighty God, the foundation and pillar of wisdom. The One who inspired me to write this book.

To my lovely sons, Edward and Edwin

Acknowledgements

"I will be glad and rejoice in thee: I will sing praise to thy name, O thou most High" (Psalm 92:2 KJV). Here comes another milestone of Grace after which the light ship survived the hurricane. Truly, the journey so far has been challenging but by His Grace I am unstoppable. I would like to appreciate Jehovah from the inner most part of my heart, for standing firm by me and remaining my help in ages past and my hope for years to come.

Most importantly also my deepest gratitude goes to my Mother, Deaconess Victoria Majekodunmi and my Father, Engineer James Majekodunmi. I want to say a big thank you for your inspirational words in bringing me up. Also, to my Father in the Lord, Prophet Adefenwa and his family, Mr and Mrs Kuku for their spiritual and moral support respectively. My appreciation also goes to my uncle, Mr Solomon Majekodunmi as well as Prophet Moses Olurin and family for their support and prayers. To my friend who acted and stood as a twin brother at the point of reality, he sheltered me during the shameful and unexpected rain, the real son of the soil, Mr Emmanuel Olusegun Akinola, you and your wonderful family shall always be remembered in my prayers and thoughts. To Prophet Larry Frank, Apostle Sheriff Jacobs, Pastor Agbaeze Okorie Ugorji, Pastor and Mrs Adelegan, Mr and Mrs Lawani, Mr and Mrs Adepelumi Agboola, Pastor Yomi Peters, Pastor Ambrose Opara and Archbishop David Fabusoro I appreciate you all for your immeasurable love and support.

To my wonderful friends Evangelist Samson Aderibigbe, Mr

John Threlfall, Ifeoluwa, Mr and Mrs Gabriel Olagbaju, Mr and Mrs Adebayo, Merrie Joy Williams, Prince Lasun Adele and family, Madam Elizabeth Giwa and Mr Odesanya. You all are wonderful and I love you all, it's my earnest prayer that higher may the Grace of the Almighty God be upon us all {Amen}. To the family of my lovely sisters {Olabimpe and Oluwabusolami} that is; the Abdulazeez and Abimbola's family, and Dr Emeka Madu. I love you both and I will forever remain grateful to God for your kinds.

To a lovely Father in Christ, Evangelist Moses Kolawole Solaru who stood beside me to instilled the required wisdom that helped me through rough times and become the man I am today, the unbeatable fact of history would foster reality and you can never be forgotten in my mind. Never would I walk pass through this side without appreciating another father, brother and friend Evangelist (Dr) Paul Babatunde Soile and his wonderful family for their passionate love and support in which mere words can't describe. My thanks likewise go to Dr. David Soile, Dr Tayo Ogunmefun, Madam Elizabeth Abimbola James and Evangelist (Dr)Richard Dele Moronfolu, Prophet Bisi Olabisi and his lovely family, Mr and Mrs Akinade for their outstanding love and words of encouragement.

I cannot forget to be grateful to my class teacher and Brother Mr Sunday Banjo and family. I would like to appreciate Evangelist Abraham O Ayoade for his professional advice. The following people have at one time or the other touched my life and I must be very thankful to them; They includes: Dr. Oluwasegun King and family whose inspired me to write this book, Dr. Deborah Titilayo Nunayon, Mr. and Mrs. A. A. Ademola, Mr and Mrs Oluyemi of Empire sports worldwide, Prophet Elijah Alabede {in blessed memory}, Madam Sheri Adekomolafe Edu, Dr. Martin Ehigianusoe will always be remembered in my little prayers for the amount of time and effort he invested in making this book a reality. I feel humbled and respected in appreciating Evangelist (Dr) Olusegun Olarinde, Evangelist (Dr) Amos

Fatusin, Mr and Mrs Apanisile, Mr and Mrs Obafaiye, Mr and Mrs Adegoke, Mrs. Alayo, Madam Fatima Tiamiyu Abioye, Pastor Samuel Donkor, John Adeyinka, Mr and Mrs Olasunkanmi Oshin, Madam Emila Adegbokun, Mr Jeremy Lunnon, Miss. Busayo Asade, Maria Olubunmi and Alhaji Olatunji Sadio for your love and contributions in making this book a reality. Mr and Mrs Oludotun Ige and Mr Samuel Ikue are all wonderful and lovely people and never to be forgotten.

Also, Philippa Gittens and her lovely family are worth to me more than any kind of treasure and I have a special place in my little heart for their encouragement which enabled me to go miles further than I thought possible. I would like to appreciate the wonderful effort of my editor and proof reader in person of Mr. Doyin Osinaike.

As l commemorate my 40th birthday with this little book to the glory of the Almighty God. I do wish myself many more years of good health, abundant wealth and a well-established life and also my family, friends, readers and well-wishers. My candid advice remains to all, as life has got nothing good in store for anyone, it's up to us as humans to search, dig deep and discover those good elements to make our lives better. Just as Oprah Winfrey said, "There is no greater gift you can give or receive than to honor your calling. It's why you were born. And how you become most truly alive". On a true note, life doesn't always give us what we want in an expected shape, but it's up to us to sharpen things to our expectations. That's why we need to do something specific for ourselves at the right time by not going where they want us to go thereby ending up at their destination. As you enjoy this book, I would advise you to take time to derive powerful insights from every chapter and paragraph to live above any form of manipulation in life. Just like Bob Marley in the track, could you be loved? Don't let them fool ya, or even try to school ya, oh, no We've got a mind of our own........... in few, never allow manipulation of any kind by not first understanding the rules of the game before playing, allowing manipulation also is as good as allowing lions to be led by donkey or the blind to lead those with two eyes wide opened. Lastly, be wise with the various choices you make in life, never take the wrong route out of sentiments and never become a victim of yourself.

Grace,

Emmanuel Goshen.

Preface

As humans, we do desire travelling from one destination to another for various reasons either visiting family's members, friends or going on an adventure. As the case might be some destinations might be far while some might be near. However, we choose the means of arriving at our valuable destination. In most cases, we prefer to travel by air to arrive at the farer one because it's considered to be faster regardless of the risk attached to travelling by air. Come to talk of travelling by air, there are two inevitable periods which are the take off and the landing period. As passengers, we commonly hope and pray to take off and land safely because regardless of the amount we purchase our flight or the technical condition of the plane both the take-off and landing periods are never within the control of any passengers and however, they can never choose what happens at take-off or landing period. In fact, these two periods rest in the hands of the pilot another unforeseen circumstances. All passengers could do all such things within those two inevitable periods, from experience, some would choose to sleep or keep to themselves, some play games, some watch movies, some read books or magazines while some would start networking or making new friends. The truth is, no matter what any passenger chooses to do within the take-off and landing periods remains their personal choice which is within their control and no one takes responsibility for another man's action within those periods. Likewise, is the life of every man, as popularly said that life is a journey and never a final destination. It's up to every one of us to choose whatever we want to be in life and where we desire as well. Imagine the take off period as our birth period, whereby it's totally out of control to choose which day to be born, what time to be delivered, where to be delivered or the name to answer. We could only at some point of our lives wish to have been given birth in a particular city or country for various reasons but we can never help it because it's outside our control. And all things being equal no man can help himself once he attains his landing point in life commonly known as the final bus stop according to the Yoruba proverbs. However, what we could do during the take-off and landing periods of our life is execute the commonest power to humans to make a choice of how we spend our lives. The more we grow, either fortunate or other way round, we remain inevitable to various challenges either internal challenges such as self-limitation or self-doubt, or external ones which originate from others or unknown circumstances of life. My point is, regardless of what the fact might be, we are to make a choice from the available alternatives in front of us i.e. either to dwell within the vacuum of mediocrity or to break out of it and live life at its fullness. Once again, the more we grow, the more we are expected to mature and depend less on others in terms of discovering ourselves, getting our direction right and attaining where we want to be in life. Bear in mind, at the beginning of every race being contested by various runners, various things are being seen and expected. Some runners could only see themselves participating, while some could only see the challenges on the track preparing them for a win or lose, leaving the potential outcome to the hand of chance and not choosing to do whatever it takes to see the possibility of winning the race. For further illustration, I would like to iron out that life is similar to a marketplace where you have to make a choice of what to buy or not. The need to make a choice or choices within the marketplace can never be underestimated because the inability to make choices at the marketplace could either amount to waste of valuable time or waste of money by buying those things which are not necessary. So is the case of anyone who can't choose whatever he wants or where he wants to be in life would have their life lived by another person without compensation. As we choose how spent our life's, regardless of the inevitable challenges we are left with to face, we either reap the reward of choosing the right thing to be done at the right time or we later face the consequences of making either the wrong choices or ignoring what ought to have being done at the right time. The reality is, success doesn't happen just because you made some clear and beautiful goals. Success happens because you wake up every single day and embrace the habits that turn big dreams into realities. According to Abraham Lincoln, "Adhere to your purpose and you will soon feel as well as you ever did. On the contrary, if you falter, and give up, you will lose the power of keeping any resolution, and will regret it all your life." In a few words, your choice today would always determine where you found yourself tomorrow.

Your Choice Either Make Or Break You

"Only you can decide what you become."
Seth Adam Smith,

When talking about choices, many takes it as if it means making decisions. In a few words, choices are personal while decisions are ourselves connected with others for a purpose. In other words, decisions are collective in nature. For instance, a manager who understands his daily task plans or list of what to be done as expected of him but chooses to carry out those tasks at his convenience because it's personal but the same manager could only decide which tasks his subordinates are to carry out within a specific time but the subordinates chooses to carry out the task or not. And irrespective of what they choose to do, the outcome remains theirs. Our ability to make the right and reasonable choices in life is what distinguishes us from the crowd. We understand that life is full of uncertainties, controversies and various forms of risk, yet we need to make a choice of how and where we want to be, else circumstances would determine or position us in life where it is always regrettable. Amidst similar alternatives which we do have such as choice of career, relationship and status we can only select one or few but not all. But let's bear in mind, the only way to overcome confusion is having the ability to make the right choice based on genuine insight or suggestion. for the fact that a choice was the best for me at a point in time doesn't mean it would be the best for my friend because our paradigm differs from each other and that's why we need to be realistic with every situation we are facing in life and whatever choices we make so as to stand the test of time and value because these are the main recipe for happiness in life. Going to school and being learned are different choices because going to school is about attendance while being learned is about having a better understanding of whatever has been taught and equipping one's mind with the right applicable information and philosophy towards discovering oneself and taking the right direction in life. Of course, one could pass all modules in school and obtaining a certificate doesn't make one intelligent. Learning would make us see more of life and discover more about ourselves because it's a lifetime phenomenon acquired. In fact, choice is whatever you accept to become into your life as a whole which amounts to your destiny in the long run and making no choice at all is more dangerous than making wrong choices. The story below throws more light on how our choices in life can either make or break us.

STORY 1:

Once upon a time, there lived a wealthy and rich king. He was known for his flawless administration as to how he ruled the hearts of his subjects. People would come to him with their problems hoping he would never send them back disheartened. Time passed, years flew by and the king started to become old and frail. He began to worry about who would take care of his kingdom after his death. The question of who would be the heir for his chair started to loom in his mind.

The king was blessed with three sons, who were loyal, obedient and respectful. But he wanted all three of them to go through an acid test in order to prove themselves and to see who possesses the real attribute of a king. So, he decided to chalk out a plan. He called his three sons and gave them 100 gold coins each and a year timeframe for a special task. Then he said, "Whoever brings a golden dog for me shall be my successor". The three sons set out with their own set of gold coins.

The eldest of three brothers went to the city and took a palace on rent for himself. Then he hired some men, and sent them in all four directions, with the order to find him the golden dog. After a few weeks, these men returned empty handed. In all of this process, his 100 gold coins got over. The eldest son lost the fight for the throne then and there. The second son became a broker in the town and started lending money to people on lower interests. He earned multiple profits through this business and with the money he had great profits, he gave the local goldsmith the order to make a Golden dog.

The youngest of all three was the wisest. He bought a small house for himself and started staying in a colony of poor and needy people. He invested his money in a business and got heavy profits from it and thereby employed a few poor people under him. He not only provided employment to the poor but also built hospitals and schools for the poor from that money, in order to help them lead a better life. Seeing his contribution to them, the poor people around him were very happy and started treating him God-like. Satisfied with his work he went back to his father

A year passed by and the three sons stood in front of the king. The eldest gave nothing; the second son gave a golden dog while the third one came. He said, "His Highness please accept this dog made out of cotton. I ask you in all humility, not to underestimate the special appeal of this dog. I have crafted it with my own hands. The hard work toil under the hot sun to grow this cotton and the labour put in by my fellow companions is nothing less than gold."

Those words and feelings of the youngest son brought tears to the king's eyes as he had felt and related himself to all the feelings of a common man, essential for a future king. In a few words, the throne was given to the youngest son for his capability and merit. However, the king was upright in his decision because the three sons were given equal chances to get the throne but their choices determined their successes and failures.

STORY 2:

A young lady worked as a primary school teacher and was well known to be the fiancée of a young man with prospects and presently the assistant manager in a soap manufacturing company. While their families and the whole community were expecting them to tie the knot, the young lady suddenly came across another man who introduced himself as an oil and gas dealer and an international investor in gold and other precious stones. Based on her weak mind-set and all the sweet talk from the businessman, she couldn't let go of the man because she had been taken out for expensive shopping and she could see everything golden for herself. She felt disturbed and she couldn't make up her mind and so she sought her aunt for advice. After so much reflection and deliberations in terms of comparing the two suitors, her aunty summarized that a dog can never have the size of a cow and she has gotten the choice to arrive at her destination by road or by air. Think and choose wisely said her Aunty.

Not long after, she got married to the business man in less than six months, after giving the assistant manager whom she dated for over five years the red card. Not quite long she became pregnant, a few months down the line, while in a heavy state, the business man told her he would be embarking on a business trip and hopes not to stay long. The following morning, she had some male visitors who came to take possession of the house where she lived with the businessman. After much struggle to prevent the possession of the house with many unsuccessful phone calls to reach the businessman. She was later shown a court order notifying the huge debt her husband was owning the bank and how he used his house as collateral. The young lady became helpless in her heavy state as the same man had also sold his cars without her consent. She eventually seeks her aunt's help who denied her any form of support claiming it was her choice and it's no one's responsibility other than hers as she did make her choice of being content with little but she chose already made wealth. After much regrets, pains and suffering, she eventually had a set of twins while she was being supported by a charity organisation, a few years later she was notified that the same man had settled issues with his former wife and moved back to his initial family. The young lady later came across the assistant manager who got promoted and eventually set up his own business, she tried to tender an apology but it was too late because the assistant manager had settled with another lady as time and tide waited for no man. It was her choice to be smart on the short run and end up losing on the long run.

Taking a review on both situations, the king's last son was able to understand what his father meant by golden dog simply because he has an empathetic heart while believing in helping others while in need. The second son was interested in playing smart and ended up reflecting a dubious character, it was crystal clear to the king that such a son can never be trusted with such a position. It was painful the first son was confused with the interpretation of what the king desires. He wasted time, effort and other resources that he empowered him. Bear in mind, none of their choices were wrong, it's only the fact that the king has to make his choice right. Coming to the issue of the young lady, I am sure she would have wished never to have placed the stigma upon herself because she ended up losing good life and enjoying a nice family which was her dream. However, the truth is, the young lady was materialistic which placed her in a swindle pit and also prevented her from making the right choice and standing by it. Sean Covey, the American author says, "Depending on what they are, our habits will either make us or break us. We become what we repeatedly do".

Our choice is what guides all our life, it is who we are and what we are known for by others. Our previous experience or background is never excusing, whatever we choose to make of our life is what matters. Such is the case with some notable people in today's world. John Paul Dejoris, the Greek-Italian-American entrepreneur, a self-made billionaire had his parents divorced when he was two, he began to sell newspapers and Christmas cards door to door at the age of nine. When his mother was no longer able to support him, he was sent to live in a foster home in Los Angeles where he joined a gang. His high school maths teacher once told him he can never be successful in anything in his life. He later became a janitor and also an insurance salesman. In a few words, John Paul Dejoris, is an entrepreneur. He was able to make a choice of doing whatever it takes to become what he is today regardless of his background and his teacher's predictions about him. Another famous person with a similar situation is Oprah Winfrey, she was given birth by an unmarried teenage mother who worked as a maid. She spent early years of her life in poverty and was so poor that she often wore dresses made of potato sacks which made other local kids teased her about it. She was molested by her cousin, uncle and family friends at the age of nine. At the age of 13 she ran away from home and at the age of 14 she had a child who died prematurely. Having gone through thick and thin of life at her early stage in life, she is today the North America first and only multi-billionaire black person. She has recorded success in many endeavours.

When Abraham Lincoln was 9 years old, his mother died of an illness. He was formally educated for a year and had to start working at an early age and give all his earnings to his father till he reached the age of 21. He also recorded some tough experiences of life, when his first love died while he was 22 and when 3 of his 4 children died all before the age of adulthood. His wife eventually suffered from mental health asylum and he also suffered from clinical depression. In his political career, he was defeated 8 times trying to be everything from a congressman to a senator to vice president. In 1860, he won the election to become president of the United States and he is now considered to be one of the greatest presidents in American history.

Another inspiring story of a serious-minded person who chose his desired life rather than following the common route is Shahid Khan. He was born into a middle-class family from Pakistan. As a child, he would build and sell radios and make his friends pay him for borrowing his comic books. At the age of 16, he moved to the United States to pursue his dream of becoming an Architect. Shahid took up his first job as a dishwasher for $ 1.20 an hour and while at the university, during his first semester he realized Architects don't make enough money and let go his dream and ended up being an Industrial Engineer. In 1978, with $16,000 from his savings and $50,000 from a loan company, he started Bumper Works which made car bumpers for customized pickup trucks and body shop repairs. Within two years, Shahid was able to buy a company he had previously worked for and merged it with Bumper Works. Not quite long, he became the sole supplier for the entire Toyota line in the United States. I would like to stress a particular point here, the main reason why many people fail in life is not all about the choices they make but how they structure the pattern of those choices into applicable and achievable plans. For instance, if Shahid had not gotten a product or service ready it wouldn't be possible to become the sole supplier of a multinational corporation such as Toyota. Many people desire to achieve greatness without getting the required platforms ready. Furthermore, to avoid limited success, Shahid worked hard to the extent of his company generating $17 million dollars in sales and later estimated $2 billion in 2010. By 2011, Shahid had 12,450 employees, 48 manufacturing plants in the US and abroad and took 3 billion in revenue. Not long after he took the biggest leap and bought the Jacksonville Jaguar for $ 760 million. Shahid, became the first member of an ethnic minority to own an NFL team and became a member of the NFL foundation. By 2013, Shahid also became the owner of the London football club Fulham F.C. However, his current net worth is over $ 7.2 billion. He was featured on the front cover of the Forbes magazine as the face of the American dream and also ranked 70th in the Forbes 400 list of richest Americans. He is also the 158th wealthiest person on planet earth and the richest person in Pakistan. He is a practical example of how a serious-minded person could choose to work out their dreams with a mind of possibilities and not probabilities. His story inspires one never to sit on the fence but join the moving train.

By and large, apart from being futuristic in terms of what he wanted and where he wanted to be in life, his choice of being realistic and not sentimental helped him live his desired life. He chooses the hard work which pays him a lot today. However, his choice to change career was the genesis of his fortune in life, many in similar situations might begin to pretend and make a cover up reflecting all to be well and later blame others, surrounding parameters and various circumstances after disappointing themselves. According to Graham Brown, Life is about choices. Some we regret, some we are proud of, some will haunt us forever. The message: we are what we choose to be. Bear in mind, there's more is lost by indecision than wrong decision because of the valuable lesson learnt.

The above-mentioned people have an inspiring story to tell the world simply because they choose to be realistic with what they wanted to be and where they wanted to be in life. They could have chosen to be sentimental and remain static in the motion of life that is, doing nothing. Their situation was transformed not because of well wishes or regular dreams but doing whatever it takes. The fact is, many have great dreams but few work out their dreams. Being honest is a choice and being sentimental is also a choice and there are measurable rewards for both. The hard core truth is, push yourself, because no one else is going to do it for you. According to Israelmore Ayivor, "There are two main predictions for the future; it's either appealing or appalling. An appealing future is created by people who identify their real values in life and believe in what they can do. Tony

Robbins, said, "In essence, if we want to direct our lives, we must take control of our consistent actions. It's not what we do once in a while that shapes our lives, but what we do consistently." This is the full message and nothing more.

The Power Of Your Choice

"Our choices... shows what we truly are, not our abilities".
J. K. Rowling

One thing l came to realize after years as a life coach and writer is that the similarity between life and leadership is that there are about decision making, however, to attain the best of both it involves getting the right done at the right time. Both parameters are both about Knowing what you want and what you stand for. The truth can't be underestimated or deprecated, the reality is, the truth bites hard and hot and that's why most people aren't compatible with it. it's our choice to either take life for what it is and create value for ourselves or ignore it and become what the society wants to be while missing it all at the end. According to the famous wrestler, Dwayne Johnson, "One of the most important things you can accomplish is just being yourself." Without any form of sentiment, this is the most powerful choice we need to make in life. As life itself is never a bed of roses but a serious platform of inevitable challenges which we face as humans and need to face them down by being courageous to turn those challenges to stepping stones and not taking them as obstacles. The truth is, people would be pleased with you if they could limit or confuse you with their deceit or make you limit yourself with ignorance rather than advising you to stand and fight for what you want in life. At times, we get castigated by others for no genuine reason but just to confuse us from treading the right path to fulfil our destinies or from making the right choice. Most people who castigate others are those who have gotten to a dead end in their lives and want others mostly the younger ones to become puppets and not their real self. I have lost count of how I have been castigated unnecessarily by those who've gotten nothing to offer themselves or for their selfish interest and end up eating their empty words in shame. The positive side is, I've got a good story for my children and grandchildren tomorrow. Get it right, negative people would only castigate you just to limit or control and later get you behind them also denying the space to be ahead of them. In a few words, if you don't know what you want in life or toying with your power to make a choice, people would give you what they have and use you to fulfil their purpose. Hadn't it been Jacob never knew what he wanted in life, Laban would have taken the best advantage of him and that's why we need to know what we want in life and need to be responsible for our intentions. In real sense of it, many prefer to settle for an average life while faking perfection just to avoid confronting and facing down tough challenges on the way. If you listen to a castigator, you are done. Another way round is, those can't fly wouldn't like to see you soar. In short, the theory of castigation is simple, those who *can't* would never wish you *get it done*.

According to Abraham Maslow, an American psychologist, in any given moment we have two options: to step forward into growth or to step back into safety. However, none of them is a crime against humanity but a choice with an outcome overtime. Apart from confusion and covetousness, lack of sufficient knowledge of a subject matter facilitates wrong choices which eventually lead to regrets in life. Choosing to buy an interesting and informative book written by a well-known author doesn't serve any value or add to one's knowledge but reading it while paying utmost attention is what makes one get the value of money being spent. At times people do like posing with books just to be seen as intelligent but whether one reads a book or possesses, it's a choice. After so much research, I realized that for anyone to live his desired life, there are two powerful parameters which influence one's choice. These are one's mind-set and those we surround ourselves with. In the aspect of our mind set, we could always apply one portion of it, either the scarcity or abundance aspects receptively. It would also be referred to as the possibility and impossibility aspect.

When talking of scarcity mind-set, people with such a mind see everything they need for their future, desired life, survival and progress in life as not available or not within their reach. They never see or hardly see anything positive about themselves, others and the future as a whole. People with such minds are rarely realistic with life because they dream and keep waiting for opportunities to locate them while sleeping on their waterbeds. They are well known for having a solution to every problem due to their sense of poor judgement and sentiments. They hardly believe that the opportunities dance with those ready on the dance floor and never wait for those yet to arrive, making the situation similar to the parable of the ten virgins. Take it or leave it, a scarcity mind-set would only keep one poor and unfulfilled as potentials are never actualized in comfort zones. According to William Jennings Bryan, "Destiny is not a matter of chance; it is a matter of choice. It is not a thing to be waited for, it is a thing to be achieved."

A scarcity mind-set is never a crime but does ease limitations on one's life and failure in the long run. We all understand that resources, capabilities, and opportunities needed to achieve great goals are unfairly distributed as many teams would always desire to win the trophy in a tournament. But it's up to those who are determined and ready to work out, not the weak minded or those with nice excuses. Coming to the abundance mind-set, challenges become stepping stones rather than an obstacle. People with such a mind-set are always the few and always keep the big picture in mind, seek support where needed as no one is too small to achieve significance according to John Maxwell in his book, The 17 laws of teamwork. Anyone with an abundance mind-set are mostly misunderstood by others and always attach both value and importance to their vision. They believe their vision is attainable and seek for ideas, tools and systems to make their dream workout. When we choose to have an abundant mind-set, we find the light of possibility in others easily which is one of the powerful dynamics in teamwork, partnerships, networking and any other strategic alliances. Most of the leaders in the business world today find it easier to expand their business empire and increase their wealth because they've a mind-set that's ready to take more positive and reasonable risks rather than remaining where they are due to unexpected circumstances or the fear of the unknown. It also facilitates intellectual development because people with such minds are open to learning and always get their knowledge expanded over time. In a nutshell, a lot could be mentioned about both mind-sets but as humans we have the free will to choose which one seems beneficial to us. In terms of those we surround ourselves with, I strongly believe that it's better we choose them wisely, rather than being chosen by people with no value and confusion.

When we surround ourselves with those who are inspired, motivated, open minded, passionate and grateful, we end up being a better version of ourselves. According to Kathy Caprino, "apart from having a huge positive impact on others and in the world as a whole, it inspired people to do things differently and never give up vision". However, they demonstrated six critical traits and behaviours that enlightens us, lighten a spark inside of us, and makes us want to be better, stronger, bigger, and more of who we are. Coming across and relating with motivated people would marginalize internal energy, renew and strengthen our determination, also our vision. From my experience, relating with motivated people enhances our ability to challenge our assumptions and think critically in line with our purpose in mind. Motivated people enable others to think in a visionary manner and participate fully in any endeavour they find themselves in life that is, optimism. When motivated, we become thirsty for more challenges and willingness to take risks increases within us. We also possess a better self-esteem with an attitude of success because we become more eager towards learning and getting things done.

In terms of being open-minded, this needs to always be on top of the list when it comes to traits and habits which we need to acquire a happy life. In other words, narrow-minded people are never able to stretch their thoughts, knowledge, and ideas beyond a self-constructed boundary that prevents them from seeing varying aspects in any situation. They often view certain actions or situations with one possible outcome and forgo all the other possibilities that could earn a positive outcome. However, this is a sure-fire way to dwell in misery forever. Open-minded people are always willing to accept responsibility for whatever outcome they get and not blaming others. They prefer to embrace change in any reasonable situation mostly when they could read future trends regarding an existing situation. However, open-minded people respect people's differences and are always open to others' opinions or ideas and never judge or talk down others. Above all, they live in the present by facing whatever they do or intend to do with a serious mind and not waiting for life to get it done for them which could face them down before thinking of alternative starting points or remedies.

People who understand their choices are well known to be excited about their goals in life, they believe in it and never compromise it for any reason. They always choose to be and remain courageous mostly in tough situations as they gain strengths and lessons in every disappointment, let downs and set back that life throws at them, they never see themselves fail when things go the opposite side but learn from their mistakes and turn them to experiences. Nothing in life makes sense other than the free will to make choices at any given time. This is what enables us to remain determined and do the needful with a positive mind, moreover, we experience growth when we are able to choose and learn from various platforms in life.

Coming to reality, the genesis of mankind had been made

and filled with various controversies at different points in time which makes the strive for significance in life a no play matter. Of course, we all desire greatness in life but it's up to us as individuals to make the right choices at various points in life. In a few words, choice is the commonest thing given to all humans. In terms of significance, we either make the choice of pursuing it till it's attained or we bury it all at the initial point or part way. Take for instance the story of the good Samaritan, according to the Bible, people who passed by the victim while half dead showed some level of sympathy but that couldn't affect the victim in any positive manner. But the good Samaritan chose to help and save the man's life by doing the needful. He could face where he was going as he was on a journey somewhere but forgot whatever he was going for to save another man's life due to the compassion he had. This was what made him one of the positive characters in the Bible. In simple terms, sympathy is just a mere feeling with no effect while compassion is taken to a certain effect or impact in any situation.

Another reflection of the power of choice is that of Jacob's. After being blessed by Isaac his father through manipulation or deception at the expense of his elder brother, Esau. He had a setback in the hands of Laban for 21 years. However, he had to make a choice at some point in life because a servant remains a servant no matter how long he spends with his master. Jacob's choice of departing from Laban's house after a critical thinking of his future made him blessed in the long run. Reading the book of Genesis 30, in the bible would give insight into why one needs to make a choice and not leaving it into the hands of chance or circumstances which is the main message of writing this book. According to Edwin Markham, 'Choices are the hinges of destiny'. In this case the term choice is never a toy-like matter and that's why if Jacob hadn't made his choice of departing Laban's house, he would have ended up wasting his life with no value in exchange for it. And such is the situation of many people till now.

According to John C. Maxwell, 'we are either the masters or victims of our attitudes'. It is a matter of personal choice. Who we are today is the result of choices we made yesterday, tomorrow we will become what we choose today. In reality, without us having a deep understanding of the power of making good choices in life, there's a huge tendency of living for no reason or under fulfilling our potential. John C. Maxwell, also said, 'Life is a matter of choices, and every choice you make makes you'. However, one of the best and powerful choices which could be made by anyone aspiring to be successful is surrounding himself with successful and confident people to enable us face our fears and break out from our comfort zones because we could become whatever we could imagine of ourselves. The power of choice is the major platform to overturn failure to success provided one could make use of available resources to kick start through planning and staying focused at the right time. Bear in mind, the right time to start creating our desires is now. The American artist, Andy Warhol, always says time changes things, but you actually have to change them yourself. A leader who is unable to exercise authority or without insight is no leader, so likewise, a man who is unable to make a choice for his own life is worthless. In a nutshell, we need to be independent and responsible for our lives by having a picture about it or we end up living another man's life. According to Earl Nightingale, "all you need is the plan, the road map, and the courage to press on to your destination". The Austrian philosopher, Viktor Frankl, also opined that "Everything can be taken from a man but one thing: the last of the human freedoms—to choose one's attitude in any given set of circumstances, to choose one's own way".

Why make choices?

Attitude is a choice. Happiness is a choice. Optimism is a choice. Kindness is a choice. Giving is a choice. Respect is a choice. Whatever choice you make makes you. Choose wisely".
Roy T.Bennett.

In life, everything is valuable only twice that is, before getting it and after losing it. Without any form of doubt, it's paramount in life we make better choices and understand the main philosophy behind every choice we make because life is a matter of sowing and reaping. According to Elisabeth Kubler-Ross, I believe that we are solely responsible for our choices, and we have to accept the consequences of every deed, word, and thought throughout our lifetime. Choices are essential to our lives, as humans, and I urge you to make sure the impact of your choice is the right one. In the works of John C. Maxwell, "Life is a matter of choices, and every choice you make makes you". Another point is, if we choose not to make a choice in any situation, there would still be an outcome but it might be disappointing. As I usually say, if we choose not to value ourselves by facing the realities of life that is; doing the needful at the right time, our choice would end at the advantage of others and their reality faces us by becoming their prey. Bear in mind, no reasonable entrepreneur would ever think of doing something for the sake of nothing and also do nothing for the sake of getting something vital and that's why we need to act and stop waiting for the perfect time. One of the great lesson l learnt from reading the leadership gold by John Maxwell, is living your life for yourself by achieving whatever you are passionate at the right period to avoid seeing yourself regretting later in life. By and large, unless we are willing and able to take full responsibility for ourselves and the choices we make, we have no control over our lives. We have been given all the power to create our experiences through our choices, but if we believe that outside forces are responsible for our choice, we give away all the power we have. Our inability to make the right choices at the right time over our lives makes the leaf blow away by the wind. According to Neal Boortz, the American author and former attorney said, "the key to accepting responsibility for your life is to accept the fact that your choices, every one of them, are leading you inexorably to either success or failure, however you define those terms." In terms of defining our choices in life, we would understand it's also a reflection of whatever we stand for in life and also an indication of our future potential. In reality, it's better we choose to be wise by standing and fighting for a good cause we desire or believe in. According to Jim Rohn, "if you spend everything you make now, you'll have no choice but to work longer and harder". But if you start investing in your financial future now, you'll have many choices. Without any form of doubt, whatever choice we make today would determine the extent we attain tomorrow. Jeff Bezos, said while sharing his experience on making the right choice. After he got the idea of selling all kinds of books online, he walked up to his boss to share his idea. After a long walk, the boss said the idea is a good one but not for someone with a good job. However, Jeff chose to give it a shot, not thinking of the number of times he might try and fail because it was a difficult choice to make. No one would ever blame the boss for his advice because he can't give what he doesn't have. Jeff was the one responsible to see the light in whatever he wants to do with his life and so likewise any reasonable person on earth. He further said, we all have choices, either to wilt under criticism or follow our convictions. In short, we either choose to build a powerful empire with our lives or waste it in the interest of others by not knowing what we want in life or taking it with levity. We need to make choices most especially when we are convinced over the need for a change at various aspects or stages in life. Dolly Parton, an American singer once said, "if you don't like the road you're on, start paving another one". I love this quote because you don't wait for others to pave a way for you if you know where you are going in life. Taking a critical review of her quote and her rag to riches life stories, one would deeply understand the impact of making better choices in life. Dolly Parton was born without a silver spoon and was dirty compared to other local children. She grew up poor and shared a room with 11 other children. Her family was poor to the extent that they couldn't afford a doctor when she had an accident where her toes were hanging before her mother had to sew it back. However, Dolly developed her passion for music by listening to radio which enabled her to create the first guitar from an old mandolin and two bass guitar strings. Due to the level of her seriousness, her uncle bought her a real guitar, she never stops singing even while washing dishes. Simply because her father saw the light in her passion, he usually drove her to present radio programmes and later on became a music star. Her father's choice of supporting her at the early stage of her career got her up the ladder and also her choice to remain consistent at what she loves doing. At times when various unexpected circumstances in life try to limit us, make us feel rejected, lock us in or place us behind, we have the choice to either follow the trends simply because we are available or make ourselves valuable and change unexpected causes in life. However, changing cause would enable us to determine those things that happen to us rather than being opened to chance. To change an unwanted cause in life, we don't need to wait till something happens, we should make efforts in making our desires happen to us. From the story of Jacob and Laban, the former had to make a choice that is, either to stay or leave before changing causes in his life. And the same principle applies till now, the inspiring story of Peter Dinklage, who once disliked himself because he felt rejected and not fitting in among his friends due to his short height. He once felt self-conscious about his appearance and also wondered what he had done to deserve such a terrible fate. As this couldn't change the situation, he chose to change the way people see him and eventually ventured into acting which made people recognize his talent and not his height. From his story, rather than accepting limitations due to his height, he chooses to press harder in terms of discovering himself towards what he could do and what he could be. And never waited for things to change but he created the change. The fact is that life doesn't give anyone his desire, it has to be worked for by whoever wants it better. In other words, it's a matter of not waiting for change to occur naturally but create the change you want to experience or see. Such was the case of Frederick Douglass, who choose to learn in the midst of slavery, after being broken, beaten and brutalized, Frederick Douglass is an undying proof that knowledge is in 0fact power. This is the remarkable true story of how a former slave used the power of words to free himself and thousands of others. Our choice is a serious reflection of our life, and that's why we need to be wiser with it. We are today the result of choices we made in our past and tomorrow we shall be the avatar of the choices we make today. We all have the choice to see and take life as a passage or as a final destination at any point. Either or, the ability to choose varies among humans and one choice can never fit all. Making better choices in life makes us value able to the dreams, goals, purpose and commitments we made to help to guide our path toward accomplishment. It would also avoid us being the traitor for your own desires. A better choice is a powerful psychological weapon which is enabled to disconnect us from negative alternatives and limitations because we are able to challenge obstacles and assumptions rather than adapting and abiding by myopic facts, life is whatever you make it to become or create out of it. In short, when life becomes a game, you play and if a battle you fight. Playing games with life when in battle is like going to a wrestling ring unprepared. Sticking to right choices can enable us to do the impossible; of course, it might attract brief struggles and failures but will always position us for greatness in life. Get it right, wrong choices shatter our lives and make us end up regretting. Also, it could also land us in total disaster and can completely destroy all our good relationships with others and this is why we should be courageous at trying again regardless of the number of times we fail. However, we would be better off if we expected more of ourselves in terms of what we could achieve or attain as a result of our hard work and determination. It wouldn't be the best of us to aim lower by settling for less or feeling comfortable with where we are. We should always believe as long as we are alive there is more in terms of what we could achieve in life. Mark Twain, once said, "Keep away from those who try to belittle your ambitions. Small people always do that, but the really great make you believe that you too can become great". Once again, our ability to think critically enables us to make better and hard choices to supersede limits and makes us progressive. This would make us not only an asset to ourselves but an opportunity to mankind and never a liability to others. In today's fast changing and controversial world, making better choices is hard which would remain tough and complicated, yet still have to be made. By and large, our destiny is never in what others say or think about us but in whatever we project and choose to do for ourselves. When asked the question on why make choices, then we need to understand the difference between living life and fulfilling life. Millions were born and lived like any other while those fulfilled are those who were dedicated in their endeavour and left behind a lasting legacy. Am always motivated by the poem Hard Choices composed by Jojoba Mansell.

GET IT RIGHT YOUR CHOICE IS YOUR DESTINY

Hard Choices by Jojoba Mansell

A path is laid out ahead, it forks before your feet.

A decision filled with dread, Uncertain of what you'll meet.

A game full of chance, Of many hidden pitfalls.

To find true romance, Dare you risk losing all?

Choices never easy to make, Fog seems to cloud your way.

You fear making a mistake, Of gambling and losing the day.

But life is full of Hard Choices, And risk is part of the game.

Be brave, ignore doubting voices, Make the choice, life won't be the same.

Drive Your World

"No one can drive us crazy unless we give them the keys".
Douglas Horton

The term driving your world simply reflects valuing and attending to what matters to us in life either career or any relationship, the opposite of this is following the crowd, ending up with them and remaining at the same point with them. Driving your world is having and exercising full control over your life, else we allow external influences to determine what we get, where we are going to be and how we end up in life, similar to the story of the frog. It was able to attain greater height into the sky without wings while its mouth was shut, which was the right thing to do but the moment the frog got distracted in terms of seeking praise, it began to fall. The endpoint of the frog was painful and that's the main lesson of the story, we can reach any height by not allowing external influences to dictate or control our actions in life. When we act on intention, we are more fulfilled regardless of the result rather than acting while confused. Driving our world is something which needs to be taken seriously because the future awaits everyone and accountability can never be escaped. As l usually say, living a life with no plans or less focus on the future and just trying to please others is the best way to waste our life. As a life coach, in my experience of working with people of various ages and status, it became clearer to me that for us to be fulfilled in life we need to have an upper edge in situations partnering to our desired future and pursue those situations with the right intensity. This happens to be one of the best choices to be made in life in order to prepare and make us undefeated in striving for what is meant for us. According to Napoleon Hill, "The man who does more than he is paid for will soon be paid for more than he does". It's up to us to make today count because whatever we see later on is what we get and taking full control of our lives reflects how much we value it which enables us to challenge our trajectory as anyone who doesn't challenge himself or herself to do more and go the extra mile is mentally dead. By and large, if we don't see ourselves as valuable no one else would and if we are not true to ourselves in terms of pursuing our vision in an unstoppable manner, no one can help us achieve that. Tim O'Reilly once said, "Pursue something so important that even if you fail, the world is better off with you having tried". It enables us to chart our own destiny and not fabricate a fake life. To iron it out, if you want better results in life, you have to learn how to make better choices and you can only make better choices only if you are in full control of your life. The frog would have made it but the choice it made wasn't good enough because the situation wasn't in its control and that's why it couldn't make it back to the sky while falling. In a few words, the benefits of being in full control of our life's includes recognizing and acknowledging our self-worth which makes it almost impossible for others to impose their intentions or ideas on us or use us for their hidden agenda. Fact be told, if we don't know what we want in life, we would be entangled by others in a systematic manner and dumped after using us without any form of appreciation. In life, being nice is good but there's always a need to place limits on whatever we give others, mostly when making sacrifices to change or fix others. It might sound great or look like a good idea but we can never succeed in helping others to attain a reasonable solution without them first having a realistic view of any unfavourable situation and also admitting there's a problem which could cause unlimited damage if not addressed at the moment. Note, people who can't see or understand their problematic situation and are ready for a change would only end up frustrating your efforts. Another point I came to realize in life is that failures, unnecessary delays and setbacks caused by those who never saw sense in your efforts or cherish your person are more painful than those we cause ourselves. However, before thinking of helping others, we ought to have driven our lives to a state of significance and be mentally strong to drive ourselves forward while carrying others along. In helping others grow, I believe it's paramount we ask ourselves this question, what's the essence of fighting for people who are comfortable with their suffering? Get it right, there's no sense or point wasting energy on things we can't control or determine. The ability to drive our world makes progressive in the way we see things around us by first discovering the light within us before helping others. For instance, some situations seen as an obstacle by others might end up being a stepping stone for us because the perception of the same situations differs from others. According to David Brooks, "almost every successful person begins with two beliefs: the future can be better than the present, and I have the power to make it so". Our ability to drive our world enables us to utilize time and do more with little resources by making us ready, fit in and embrace necessary changes as success remains the outcome of preparation meeting opportunity just similar to the story of the ten virgins in the Bible. In life, what we pay attention to determines our experiences and that's why we need to choose the direction we drive our life towards rather than allowing external influences to determine our experiences or projections that is, who we are going to be, where we are going and how we end up in life. The remarkable Nigerian novelist, Chinua Achebe, did write, "Nobody can teach me who I am, you can describe parts of me, but who I am - and what I need - is something I have to find out myself". Leaving a car to move without any form of control would create a chaotic situation, so likewise our valuable life, we need to be in control of it and all attached to it. I understand the fact that avoiding some distracting temptation in life is hard but yet whatever situation we fail to handle would eventually mishandle us and land us in shame. Driving our world is a matter of having the ability to control our behaviours, emotions and also our thoughts so as to be able to plan for the long term and not the moment. It's a reflection of having a strong and sound mind because we are able to think alright and do the needful to avoid weakness, laziness, frustration and negativity dime our future. Having the ability to control our minds makes us masters of our destiny and helps us generate the willpower and positive energy to go the extra mile in any chosen endeavour. We avoid being short of ideas or stagnation, being optimist i.e. confident about the future and have the true ability to follow our dreams by pushing ourselves beyond limits if we could master our mind and not failing due to external circumstances like the funny frog. Failure to drive our world would make us see and equal the future with past failures. what a pitiful situation? Having an idea of what to do is not enough but all that matters is doing the right thing at the right time to attain desirable results with the same idea to make it valuable. Choosing to do nothing or leaving the future to chance creates more damage than making mistakes because we learn and grow this way. There are two primary choices we could make in life, either to accept conditions as they exist or accept responsibilities for changing them. People who drive their world are those with impactful and quality behaviours such as assertiveness, ambitious, strong willed, decisive, enthusiastic, charming, persuasive, patient, stable, consistent and being a good listener. People who find it difficult or impossible to drive their world are well known to be aggressive, demanding, egotistical, bossy, confrontational, easily distracted, selfish, poor listener, impulsive, resistant to change, passive, unresponsive, slow, stubborn, critical, picky, fussy, hard to please and a pretending perfectionist. Be fully aware, we are responsible for whatever we make out of ourselves either we are in charge or we allow others to drive us at our expense. Either we choose to be realistic or sentimental regarding the numerous challenges we face in life. In driving our world, we could either be a liability {always depending on and blaming others for expectations and outcomes}, an asset {self-sufficient} or an opportunity {being a blessing to one's self and others]. We need to determine and choose those we associate with and be careful of naysayers because they have nothing significance to offer rather than deceit and pretence. For us to drive our world, we need to be smart, focus and plan ahead of possible situations mostly regarding things that add value to our life, else we keep exposing ourselves to friendly manipulators who makes our situation similar to the kite in the air whose direction is determined by the wind and its height determined by the holder. Lest we forget, we need to be the main architect of our own destiny and also act with understanding while dealing with issues concerning our lives, else we would find ourselves entangled like the kite left with no choice than to follow the existing paradigm. To drive our world simply means having the audacity to live our possible best without fear or sentiments meaning that, rather than giving up we seek the courage to ask relevant questions to get relevant and applicable answers which are the real solutions. This enables us to be a real version of ourselves rather than a comfortable copycat, it also enables us to grow as we learn with the application of understanding as a whole rather than being confrontational over any misunderstandings or arguments. Les Brown, one of the American motivational speakers and author, "Be willing to go all out, in pursuit of your dream, ultimately it will pay off, you are more powerful than you think you are, Go for it". Above all, life is similar to a jungle where we have to fight and dominate or we hide and get evaporated, the choice is ours but the more we are able to drive our world, the more we are able to create our own success story and not just listen or admire that of others. Benjamin Franklin did make it clear, "without continual growth and progress, such words as improvement, achievement, and successes have no meaning". In a nutshell, in driving our own world towards living a fulfilled life, we shouldn't worry ourselves about what others are doing because this is a bad use of our creative energy, rather we should focus our thoughts and attention on our own life.

In terms of driving your world there are three categories in which we only choose to become one of in life i.e. either a liability, an asset or an opportunity. Liability are those with no positive impact to themselves and others in most cases they use and dump others claiming to be smarter than them. They are always more problems and zero solutions in any situation. They believe in waiting for luck rather than working out a real vision for themselves and live a fulfilled life. They are the ones who would wait unnecessarily at the door to open naturally while an opportunity would make some effort to get it open and also take control of the situation. In few words we are only in control of our lives when we can make choices by thriving for what we want and not waiting endlessly for them. Liabilities are those who grew old without growing up in terms of facing the reality of life, having their mouths faster than their brains. Those who attained no significance talk less of adding value to others. Liabilities are those who would criticize the performance of others without learning anything new or creating value for themselves. They are well known for carrying out instructions or activities without paying attention to details and end up making costly mistakes. Liabilities are those who castigate others easily for their selfish interest by cheating others for temporary gains with the use of negative justifiable wisdom and take revenge at others in light of mistakes rather than taking insights which later hinder their progress and prosperity in life. They are the ones who believe in the slogan of what would be would be while expecting magic or a pie in the sky rather than taking action. The best way to treat a liability is letting them go their way as they have nothing to offer and absolutely a rip-off. Rather than working hard for what would make them fulfilled in life they prefer settling for what would give temporary relief. They've no value for time and life as they are absolutely wasteful. According to Abraham Lincoln, "And in the end, it's not the years in your life that count. It's the life in your years." In reality, liabilities are the ones who would wait unnecessarily at the door to open naturally while an opportunity would make effort to get it opened and also take control of the situation by asking what next do I need to do? Liabilities are those good at pretending to be nice or good at pleasing people without planning for themselves which results in total failure, the truth is, their lack of potentials made them what they are. In a few words we are only in control of our lives when we can make right choices. Due to their lack of insights and potential they envy others achievements and try to bring others down to their level. Instead of learning the right and applicable principle to improve themselves, having gotten a better understanding of success requires they prefer to act in cheap sentiments. Rather than working hard towards becoming an asset and building a valuable future for themselves, they prefer to remain comfortable sitting on the fence watching others getting things done. They also prefer to settle for a number of bricks rather than thriving for a well-deserved mansion due their lazy mind or mentality. Assets are the ones useful to themselves and not others or having little to offer. They could go a few miles but never the extra mile because they lack the support of others such as networking or teams. Assets hardly leave their comfort zones based on the level of their ignorance or the fear of facing possible tougher challenges. Assets are commonly known to wait for someone to act first before they move as they lack vital leadership traits. They need mentors to help them think logically and critically to go the extra mile. Assets need to familiarize themselves with the act of thinking outside the box to face down challenges and become a better version of themselves. They need mentors to help withstand pressure during transformational periods. They need encouragement or motivation in the aspect where persistence is required of them which happens to be a breakthrough formula (another book to watch for). Knowledge is essential to succeed in life as life itself is about intelligence and not excuses or sentiments. Assets need to be determined to achieve the unexpected and to sustain and to be established. Assets are like birds without feathers if without mentors. To produce their best possible assets, assets need to avoid trying to be in the good books of others but sick to the right thing to be done at the right time, by learning to make their own decisions or choices in all they do. Also needs to be assertive in order to track their gradual progress and identify the need of adjustment in all aspects of their lives. They need to be sensitive in terms of they hear and listen to before making choices in any aspect of their lives, also take insight and advice from those who've done it or gone the extra mile. Above all, assets need to take insight and draw from the experience from those who have established themselves as an authority in desired direction to become an opportunity. Opportunities are those who are of a huge positive impact and inspiration to themselves and others. They act intentionally because they have a cue of whatever they want to achieve before going for it. They've gotten a lot to offer in terms of adding value to themselves and others. Those in this category strongly believe in the use of mental strength to imagine the possibility of overcoming unexpected challenges which also creates the platform for them to go the extra mile in any endeavour. Unlike liabilities who would never dare to give a trail and end up settling for less or cheap alternatives. One thing admirable about opportunities, no matter the pressure they face they never live the life created by others. Also, they support others to grow and gain their support to go the extra mile. It's possible to grow from a liability to an asset and from an asset to an opportunity via changing the cause we stand for i.e. our choice in terms having greater aspirations and acting with are fined determination to give it whatever i.e. facing down the numerous challenges with what it takes and not faking it. It's paramount we understand the fact that we can hardly overcome whatever unpleasant situation we don't confront. In short, an opportunity person has no time to waste as they act purposefully and talk less of showing interest in what's not profitable. This ideology of understanding the category we belong to is essential and the type of relationships we manage because in life we must know what we want and what we are doing as we are coming in from the cold. It takes a lot to become an opportunity to oneself and others mostly in the aspect of dedication and loyalty towards one's ambition in life. Get it right, mingling with idiots and hypocrites doesn't necessarily make us one, because we could choose to study their unpalatable manners and do the opposite or do exactly what they do and be like them. According to the American vlogger and media personality, CT Fletcher, "I don't need you to agree with me, I have the courage to stand alone." The genuine fact is, great lessons could be learnt from failures by doing what they refuse to do at the right time. Above all, the words of liabilities are parked with limitations and destruction, assets are full of knowledgeable words, while those of opportunities are loaded with insight for real direction and life. Which of those are you? Every reasonable trader would like to buy for a good discount and sell for a premium, so likewise in life we are all traders and that's why we only get whatever we make ourselves available for, the truth is, we are either available for a valuable or ridiculous price. Drive your world by determining who you should become mostly in the mist of challenges without any form of deceit this is the best loyalty anyone could give himself because a man who can't drive his world and get things done can never lead others successful and that's why the need to persist without any form compromise and this fact can't be under emphasized. Truth be told, most great people have achieved their greatest success just one step beyond their greatest failure, according to Napoleon Hill. In simple words, we should learn to drive our world and avoid been pushed by others like a push truck and later make us face the penalty for our failures.

Set Peak Standards

"The quality of a leader is reflected in the standards they set for themselves".
Ray Kroc

A little boy in primary one once scored seven out of ten sums and was so excited, his teacher questioned the reason for excitement.

Little boy: Oh, I scored a better grade

Teacher: And what made you think so?

Little boy: 7 of 10 is a good score, of course I tried.

Teacher: But you never meet the target!

Little boy: And what was it?

Teacher: 10 of 10 and nothing less.

Little boy: Ohhhhhh

Teacher: I know you've prepared your mind for an average target and that's why you are being lazy and happy.

Little boy: what can I do?

SET PEAK STANDARDS

Teacher: working hard and meeting the target.

So likewise, in life, we shouldn't just aim for existing like most people are aiming and settling for a low or average life. We should aim higher by setting a higher standard for ourselves and working it out. We need to put in our peak performance in any good cause and operate aiming for a higher target no matter our current situation. The gospel truth is this, when an adverse situation tries to limit us or lock us in our comfort zone, we still have the choice of accepting the paradigm or creating ours. We still have to choose either to be and remain mentally strong and adapt the right and applicable philosophies towards becoming a better version of who we are today or accept whatever circumstances that comes our way that is, what would be would be. From the above illustration, the little boy had seen scoring seven sums right as his peak performance and was excited hitting it but because the teacher discovered that and helped him adapt a different philosophy for his personal growth and development aiming at raising his standard for a higher one his orientation changed and saw the need to aim higher than before. When we lower our standards, we lower our quality of life as a whole. If we accept things the way it occurs, and do not change for the better, life would force us to be content with the lowest possible version of ourselves, mostly when we could do more. One thing I would like to stress here is when we desire to be a better version of ourselves, the more we focus on problems the more problems we see and remain the same or backwards but when we focus on possibilities the more likely we are to find more opportunities and be progressive in life. Whichever one we go for is our choice, either we were brainwashed, confused or blindfolded or no one shares the dancing floor with us at the point of reality. When talking of changing our lives for the better version of it, we need to first embrace the act of learning. Truth to be told expressly, if we are not willing to learn, no one can help us. But if we are determined to learn, no one can stop us from being better than what we used to be.

Tony Robbins once said *"If you want to change your life you have to raise your standards"*. Back to the illustration of the little boy in person of my first son Edward, who was later able to record a peak level of improvement simply because his teacher made him raise his standard which also reflected the effort of the teacher in the long-run. Another point we need to understand is, we would be more disappointed later in future for the things we didn't do such as taking steps out of our comfort zone. That's why we need to leave our comfort zone by raising our standard and do what you have to do without thinking of what others might say or feel about us because we've got one life to live and it's either we utilize it or waste it. When setting our personal standard, we shouldn't neglect the need for clarity and precision to avoid confusion mostly in the aspect of planning and executing our visions. Accuracy and relevance are also important parameters to be considered to make goals or vision significant and realistic.

Jack Canfield once said, *"what others think about you is none of your business"*. In the real sense of it, there's no reason to apologize for having high standards, people who really want to be in your life will have to raise theirs as well as there's nothing glorious or meritorious in playing small or displeasing ourselves for the sake of others. High standards distinguish and place value on us and not make us common or replaceable. Also bear in mind, making regrettable decisions or mistakes for the sake of those who have nothing significant to offer or later value our effort is not worth it. Jennifer Lopez, the American singer, said, *"I have my own high standards for what I want in a partner and how I want to be treated. I bring a lot to the table. I'm not talking about material things but what I have to offer as a person i.e. love and loyalty and all the things that make a good relationship"*. In my findings, people who feel negative about those striving for peak achievements and see them as potential threats and would hardly support them because they know their paradigm might not remain the same as theirs who are social pretenders living a fake life i.e. being a copycat.

The unbeatable fact remains, the more focused and reasonable we become about our lives, the less we get distracted by meaningless situations or others in our life such as unproductive arguments or valueless conversations. Setting standards makes us grow both intellectually and emotionally to realize that not everyone in our life is worth confrontation and not all issues are worth attending to. It's also about having a clear reflection of us understanding our priorities by going for the right thing at the right time and also preparing ourselves for the long-term and not the short term. I do hear people say 'you have to fake it till you make it' . In reality, such people are never true to themselves and their goals, can the foundation meant for a bungalow be used to erect a high-rise? We can only achieve what we are prepared for. For us to be successful, we need to be principled with the way we relate with others by making our time valuable, our energy priceless and waste no time with people who don't deserve them.

Extracting from Bob Marley, *"the problem is people are being hated when they are real, and are being loved when they are fake".* Furthermore, setting peak standards for ourselves in life is more about stepping out and operating outside of our comfort zone while others choose to remain or be limited/controlled by what they see, feel or assume about themselves or circumstances in life and also being an authentic version of ourselves. To hit home, when we are real to ourselves, we discover more about ourselves and aim higher, rather than criticising others who are busy doing the needful, we need to join the train and remain persistent regardless of challenges or the numbers of recorded failures. Rather than giving up and remaining the same, we would be better remaining unstoppable. Maya Angelou, the American poet, once said, *"Nothing can dim the light which shines from within".* To iron this quote, we are the only ones who can fix ourselves to stagnation. If we want to operate at a high standard, we can beat down our nice tendering excuses rather than allowing them to beat us and fix us in our comfort zones because once we become fearless, we become limitless.

According to the former American basketball player, Michael Jordan, "you have competition every day because you set such high standards for yourself that you have to go out every day and live up to that". The moment we understand ourselves and our purpose in life, apart from the various challenges we face, we own the attitude of maintaining a high standard. It's something we need to work for and not just wishing or hoping for. It would be wise of us if we don't wait for things to get easier, simpler or better. Life will always be complicated and waiting unnecessarily would only make us waste our life and nothing more. Another fact I wish to stress is the use of our mind towards placing or aiming for various standards in life. Bruce Lee once said, "If you always put limits on everything you do, physical or anything else, it will spread into your work and into your life, there are no limits, there are only plateaus, and you must not stay there, you must go beyond them". In a few words, setting our standards higher or lower is more psychological and not situational. If we are more psychologically positive, the more we become mentally strong and break through obstacles, barriers or personal imposed limits. But if psychologically negative, our minds become weaker and allow various situations to turn barriers and cage us in our comfort zone. It takes having a stronger mind to emancipate from living or existing in vacuums. Setting standard goals is the first step in turning invisible into visible, nothing more or less. It's the major recipe for setting the right goal or vision for our lives, believing in it and striving for it before achieving it. I do remember many years ago while playing the fool, my uncle Mr Samuel Ikue, did advise me saying: the farmer with a blunt machete would eventually regret at day break and that's why we are better off choosing our desired life and setting our standard by which we live at the right time. The more we wish well for ourselves, the more we need to sharpen our destinies by working towards it. a school leaver who wishes

SET PEAK STANDARDS

to become a medical doctor would have to sit and pass his school leaving examination by first studying hard ahead, make his way to medical school, learn and get examined on a number of occasions before getting qualified after meeting the expected requirements and not just wishing while the days go by. Such a student needs to value his dream by keeping his aspirations alive and remain self-motivated towards achieving his goal in life. In fact, wishing alone is meaningless without the right action in place at the right moment.

According to Henry David Thoreau, the American poet, *"Success usually comes to those who are too busy to be looking for it"*. To keep the ball rolling, setting a higher standard for our life is about having the courage to stand and fight for our desired life, having the strength to go for it and not giving excuses or living with fears. It includes discovering our direction and treading our real path in life with little or no support. When we raise our standards, it becomes possible to surround ourselves with those who talk about visions and ideas and execute them for real change. In fact, raising our standards makes us tell the story to be told by others and not the storyteller of others.

Truth be unleashed, the best alternative for turning tougher challenges to stepping stone is by first adopting genuine philosophies of the paradigm facing us and possible approaches to sort things out with positivity and create reasonable options. Benjamin Franklin said, *"Without continual growth and progress, such words as improvement, achievement, and success have no meaning"*. Setting peak standards is seriously challenging as it involves moving courageously while in an uncertain state and achieving the needful by making use of the peak of our abilities rather than waiting for life or others to place us in a state of no option while ending up under-actualizing our potentials. According to Robin S. Sharma, *"we grow fearless when we do the things we fear"*. Bear in mind, there's nothing new in the birth of anyone but the value which we are able to produce out of our life is what distinguishes us. Raising our standards strengthens and renews our determination towards achieving anything worthwhile.

As William Ernest Henley, did write in one of his poems, Invictus, It matters not how straight the gate, How charged with punishments the scroll, I am the master of my fate: I am the captain of my soul. In a few words, people with a higher standard are able to see beyond and go through the pain they bear in any adverse situation because they are sure of the victorious moments ahead. Similar examples are wrestling and boxing, in most cases, the winner might have suffered a lot of beating or punches but they refuse to give up because they value the victorious moments more than what they are experiencing during their challenging periods. I was surprised watching the WWE WrestleMania 30 April 6, 2014 which was staged, the match staging Dave Bautista, Randy Orton and Daniel Bryan. No one would have imagined that Daniel Bryan had gotten the best and most beating of his lifetime, also got up from the mobile stretcher while on his way out of the venue and later won the tournament because he considered the trophy is more valuable than the pain. The simple truth is, his standard fuelled his determination which made him not quit the match. The fact is, it was difficult while he was beating and painfully laying down hopelessly but it would have been more regretful for him not to get back into the ring and achieve his desire.

One thing I have learnt over the years is that mentally strong and successful people mightn't have attitudes but they've gotten standards. Setting higher standards is painful but enduring it is highly rewarding and worthwhile. And we can only take one of two pains in life, the pains of discipline while getting things done or the pains of regretting for not doing the needful at the right time. Kevin Hart, the American comedian, once said, *"No matter what, people grow. If you choose not to grow, you're staying in a small box with a small mind-set. People who win go outside of that box. It's very simple when you look at it"*. And that's why we need a coach or a mentor to put us through. Set-

SET PEAK STANDARDS

ting a peak is not a crime and would never be as it costs nothing to think bigger than what we are today and go for it while it costs more than a fortune to think less of ourselves in terms of what we could become tomorrow. So let's start thinking big and aim higher. Erica Williams Simon, once said the best career advice that I can give: "don't ever attach yourself to a person, a place, a company, an organization or a project, attach yourself to a mission, a calling, a purpose only, that's how you keep your power and your peace".

Choose To Be Enlighten

"Don't go through life, grow through life".
Eric Butterworth

Once upon a time, a wealthy man died unexpectedly without a will but survived by a young son and a grown-up servant. After the unexpected death of the wealthy man, there was serious controversy within the town on how the slave should be rewarded for his long-term stewardship. The servant whom had gotten a lot of friends within the same town were giving him various advices as in what to request for his long-term stewardship while the wealthy man's son whom can hardly differentiate his left from right man was amazed that his fathers' servant would have a share of his fathers' belongings which should be his inheritance. He then seeks for advice from one of the elders in the town as the big day approaches. It was a big public event as it was agreed that the wealthy man's belongings would be read out for both son and the slave to make choices. After the long list of belongings which included a male servant was made public for the purpose of transparency. The wealthy man's son requested for his father's male servant himself. The bottom line is, everything which belongs to his servant belongs to the master's son. If the young man had chosen other items and the servant was able to make a fortune from his father's properties, he would later become a threat to him within the town. The servant had no choice than to follow suit but he was ignorant of the fact that no matter how long he stays in his master's house he remains a servant. For the fact that he was well known within the town doesn't convert his status and his entitlement was discretionary and not mandatory. It would have been the best to claim his freedom at the death of his master but made his choice out of sentiments and covetousness hoping for a pie in the sky. Just as Doug Baldwin said, "The greatest tragedy for any human being is going through their entire lives believing the only perspective that matters is their own". If he was enlightened, he would have understood the fact that a servant could be sold countless times and a servant would always live his life for the purpose of his master till the day he claims his freedom. As told in a negotiation class, when bragging with the devil protect your soul because it's not replaceable and when swinging with sharks never smell blood, else you are done.

Similar to the story of Jacob in the bible, which was mentioned earlier on. But in Jacob's case, Laban's children have begun to pass complaints regarding the possibility of Jacob having a lion share in their father's wealth. Am sure if Jacob wasn't enlightened and futuristic enough to know what he wants in life which was to provide for his own house and understand why he needs to depart Laban's house after 21 years. He would have ended up serving Laban's children as well, if not for the right choice he made. But simply because he was enlightened to understand the fact that all sweet things must come to an end, he never waited for the right time, which many mistakenly do, he created his options and made the best choice which later led him to his destiny which turns out to be a point of fulfilment. I would like to state categorically that I was inspired to write this book after reading the story of Esau and Jacob. A lot of insight could be realized from the same story but the fact is that, apart from making choices to be successful in life, making choices with a huge enlightenment for a better tomorrow is what matters most. In life, we need to understand why we live and what makes us unique and discover what would make us stand out from the rest of us to be a model to others. It's good to be educated but it's limited in the long run, being enlightened exposes one to life beyond education. Enlightenment is a source of insights which aids our vision or imagination to be actualized in any aspect of life, while education is narrowed to specific knowledge and information regarding any academic subject. Zig Ziglar, the American motivational speaker, did make it clear, "If you can dream it, then you can achieve it". You will get all you want in life if you help enough other people get what they want.

Eric Butterworth once said, "seeing isn't believing, believing is seeing, you see things not as they are but as you are". The mistake of the servant was that he saw things for himself and not the way things are. He was sentimental and that's why he waited for the assumed right time rather than claiming his freedom at the death of his master. I am sure, if he was to be given another chance to make a request he would choose to be free and leave on the spot but it was late. The servant was ignorant of the writing on the wall and the truth regarding whom he was and eventually missed his way out of slavery. Kevin Harrington, the founder of As Seen On TV, being born into poverty does not mean you are condemned to spend the rest of your life in poverty. This is simply the truth but when enlightenment is missing, we end up making regrettable choices and living for the purpose of another man while we shift the blame on others for our failure. Steve Jobs once said, "your time is limited, so don't waste it living someone else's life". Don't be trapped by dogma - which is living with the results of other people's thinking. Don't let the noise of others' opinions drown out your own inner voice. And most importantly, have the courage to follow your heart and intuition because if you want to build wealth and be successful, you first need to have the right mentalities.

As we live and grow as humans, we should at least not forget this truth. Our thoughts are the framework of our actions and without the act of enlightenment, we have a huge tendency of seeing life from an adverse angle. The act of enlightenment enables one to think deeply before acting and avoids regretting at the end of our lives as a whole. Enlightenment attaches values to our life because of its capability to convert ideas to reality and attain a high level of actualization. According to Norman Cousins, "the biggest source of motivation are your own thoughts, so think big and motivate yourself to win". As I usually say, if anyone would choose to succeed in life, such should succeed big and not limited. Truth be told, in life, death is not the greatest loss in life, the greatest loss is what dies inside of us while we live. In reality, it takes enlightenment to discover those things in us and how to bring them to reality. The world would never celebrate those ideas inside of us until we bring them to reality. It's our responsibility to channel our mind in the right manner to think positive. According to Elon Musk, the CEO of Tesla, who once said, ``Really, the only thing that makes sense is to strive for greater collective enlightenment". Brandon Hendrickson also said and I quote, "the mind is stronger than the body. Trust that and watch what your body can do". An enlightened person would never allow excuses to tie them in their comfort zone which is a reflection of fear and laziness. The reality which we need to understand as we grow day in and out is, life as a whole has got two choices for everyone which is to make everyone equal and it's up as an individual to plan and focus on being equipped with the right insight towards discovering ourselves and chart our course in life. In fact, life is whatever we make it become, either to sit, sulk and dwell on how life has been unfair or we control the various situations facing us and turn it around in our favour. Lori Deschene, don't let your fear paralyze you. The scariest paths often lead to the most exciting places.

For the purpose of an in-depth analysis, comfort zones make one feel safe and in control while at the lowest ebb of one's life in which many remain or position themselves at this point due to induced orientation by someone in the form of brainwashing or personal imposed limitation or belief. These are those who think of moving or in a specific direction but wish others to like them. People do keep to this state while imagining the impossible i.e.

creating bogus hopes till they become hopeless such as the servant mentioned easier on. According to Pele, "Success is no accident. It is hard work, perseverance, learning, studying, sacrifice and most of all, love of what you are doing or learning to do". It also includes acquiring new skills and not just depending on one's previous knowledge because the global paradigm changes and learning something new enables one to break out of our comfort zone and remain irreplaceable. Success involves setting new goals with a higher standard after attaining previous ones to avoid limitations and be outdated. By and large, Bill Richardson, the American diplomat, Ignorance has always been the weapon of tyrants; enlightenment the salvation of the free. In a nutshell, our choice to be enlightened empowers our freedom of expression rather than being encompassed by an unknown scheme.

Choosing to be enlightened makes us teachable and gain more than we could have lost, the more we become open to new ideas, that is, ways of thinking and seeing the paradigm shift. In business for instance, lack of new ideas could put one into the hands of the competitor because one being able to manufacture a product and get it to the marketplace doesn't give the manufacturer the legal right to impose it on the customer because no manufacturer can deny the customer the right of making choices. To remain hale and hearty in the marketplace, a real business would need to study the market trends before developing a new fashion or the taste of the customer or create a new product or service. Enlightenment is a powerful weapon to control our emotions and overcome daily challenges. It helps make right choices and avoid being explored unexpectedly. It also enables us to live a desirable life or otherwise be forced to live a frustrating one, in short, lack of enlightenment makes us slaves of our past and irrelevant for the future. Jim Rohn once said, "Humans can turn nothing into something, pennies into fortune and disaster into success." In a nutshell, without enlightenment, nothing remains nothing and we see things the same way as others. Bear in mind, zero plus zero would always remain zero, if a good idea is not well communicated or structured to produce, it would never produce value. It takes one who is enlightened to discover the silver lining in every experience no matter how dull the shine.

The truth is, everything we need is already inside of us, there's no point waiting for others who don't have a clue of what we want in life to light our candles when we have gotten our matches. Instead of waiting for such people, it's better we seek the right support and surround ourselves with those who have gotten real insights and are interested in us being a better version of ourselves with the aid of their ideas and experiences to enable us to grow intellectually. When we desire to be more enlightened, we need to understand the fact that it's a gradual process and not magic. Idries Shah once said, Enlightenment must come little by little - otherwise it would overwhelm. We need to ask the right questions to get the right answers. Enlightenment requires knowing how to reserve our judgment until we have all the facts regarding a particular subject matter and to challenge existing assumptions aiming at expanding our desire to know more. Buddha said that enlightenment was the end of suffering, and that only at that point will we know true happiness. To be enlightened, is to be progressive in life regardless of hardships being faced. If obstacles were to be removed no man would move forward.

The fact is, obstacles have been in existence from the world go and will always remain but it's up to us to make a choice either to make it stop or we get over it. In life, situations which are attached to insult, frustration, rejection, failure and mistakes are always and would always remain inevitable on the way to success but if enlightened we would never be devastated and depressed at any of them. One thing I would like to iron out, great people of today, once suffered the uncalled-for situation in life. Michael Jordan after being cut from the high school basketball team, he went home, locked himself in his room, and cried but later on to become a legend in the world of the same game.

GET IT RIGHT YOUR CHOICE IS YOUR DESTINY

Oprah Winfrey was once demoted from her job as a news anchor because she was considered not fit for television but later went on and became one of the greatest TV personalities. The Beatles were rejected by Decca recording studios, with the statement "we do not like their sounds, they have no future in the shoe business" but went on and breakthrough in the world of music. The fact is, enlightenment would always overcome limitation if we are strong, seriously minded and persistly courageous. One thing that is common among them is failure but they still went on to exercise the power of their choices either to fall back or carry on. As Winston Churchill, "Success is not final, failure is not fatal: it is the courage to continue that counts". It's good to pray and wish ourselves well but the best only comes when we choose to work out with a high level of enlightenment.

Get it right, enlightenment enables us to train our mind to be stronger than the challenges we face, to avoid losing ourselves at any point in life. It enables us to avoid taking issues personally but take comments or criticism in a constructive way. And also ask ourselves if there is any truth in the comments or criticism and also learn from the situation to become a better version of ourselves and not be defined by any adverse situation in life. It takes enlightenment to know that we cannot please everyone mostly when in a leadership position but can bridge a gap. In critical and challenging moments, being enlightened enables us to take a different perspective, reason in a critical way and ask ourselves real questions in an unbiased manner to enable us to lead others and not wait to be directed by others as a result of confusion. According to Margaret Thatcher, don't follow the crowd, let the crowd follow you. Louis Leo Holtz, the former American football player, coach, and analyst, once said, Ability is what you're capable of doing. Motivation determines what you do. Attitude determines how well you do it. In a few words, it takes being enlightened to discover what we're capable of becoming in life and desire more. To be successful in life, it's wise to search for the causes of failure and learn from them before making moves. And being enlightened enables us to see challenges as stepping stones and not what people take it to be, we need to understand one thing in life, without rain nothing grows and for the sake of bountiful harvest i.e. a bright future, we should learn to embrace the storms anytime.

One thing I could iron out from my personal experience is that, it's better to be fulfilled in life rather than to be rich. Being fulfilled could enable riches to last longer but being rich alone could last a short while. One could be rich by opportunity but a change could affect the situation in a negative manner. My point is, being enlightened makes us desire the right thing at the right time and not doing things in exchange for short-term reward. It enables us to make choices based on the right and accurate insight and not by sentiments and facilitates growth for a better standard of living and relating with others. Truth be told, in life we're either growing or declining, when we grow, we move upward the spiral and begin to experience joy, freedom, love, passion, enthusiasm, hope, eagerness, happiness, optimism, belief and positivity. Otherwise, the outcome would be frustration, impatience, worry, rage, jealousy, insecurity, irritation, doubt, anger, hatred and guilt. However, being enlightened enables us to overcome challenges rather than creating flip excuses and living a desirable life and not living each day the way it comes.

Enlightenment is a strong key that prevents us from giving up our ambition by helping us focus on fulfilling our vision and not the pain attached towards achieving it. The inspirational story of Laurence Tureaud, popularly known as Mr T is a typical reflection of why we need to be enlightened in life. Laurence Tureaud, was the youngest of 12 kids and he knew he had to toughen up to achieve his desired lifestyle. He was enlightened enough not to settle or survive for just a livelihood but thrive for a befitting lifestyle and had to give what it takes and not create excuses. He ventured into bodybuilding by training countless hours a day due to fear of his own safety. His discipline and ability to focus and to remain strongly determined enabled him to train and excel in martial arts, football and wrestling. During his active days in the ring, he won the championships back-to-back. According to him, "you're going to face adversity, the main thing is don't quit, that's what separates the winners from the losers". With all his potentials he later ventured into acting but faced various challenges as he often landed him in minor parts. But still persisted in his wrestling career which later got him noticed by a famous actor and featured in the movie Rocky lll. After an audition, Sylvester Stallone became impressed at his performance and decided to change the script with the aim of giving more lines. Playing the role of the ruthless Clubber Lang, he was positioned for a big break which was the TV series, A Team where he played the iconic tough guy BA. In a few words, Mr T continued to wrestle throughout his acting career and was later recognized at the WWE HALL OF FAME. Today, Laurence is an advocate for young people and worked on various anti-drugs campaigns. He also released a musical album on making good choices and also travels round the world motivating others to never stop chasing dreams of their desirable lifestyle. Mr T, once said, "I pity the fool who just gives up because you never lose until you stop trying". From Laurence's story, it's crystal clear that perseverance is one vital key in achieving greatness in life. However, focusing on the pain or hurt will cost us to suffer the most, but focusing on the lesson will make us grow the more. People with no understanding of our projected future wish to see ourselves the way they see us. And if we are not properly enlightened, we would grant them the access to control our journey and at the end miss our destination.

    As generally said, to be informed is to be transformed and to be uninformed is to be deformed. The more enlightened we are in any life cause or subject matter, the more we command respect. However, this has nothing to do with age or any other status. As we move on in life, it's paramount we get enlightened mostly in any desirable direction and not pretending to be what we aren't or yet to be. Being enlightened enables us to reflect value in our actions, relationship with others and how we execute and drive our vision to the point of accomplishment. We are able to apply wisdom and knowledge in the right manner and channel to stabilize our destiny which guarantees sustainable success as a whole. We can be deeply enlightened by reading books of authorities in our respective fields or great leaders who tried and failed various times before accomplishing greatness. And without beating around the bush, readers today are leaders tomorrow. According to Bishop David Oyedepo, "ignorance is costly, don't toy with it". The same way we make life what we want it to be, the same way we make our challenges either our mountain or stepping stones. Nothing great in life is meant to be easy, we just have to fight for it. The truth is, there are no obstacles or mountains in reality other than our ignorance that is, our mentalities. Above all, we should be willing to learn. Mentally strong people do not see learning as a tedious process, but as an essential routine to develop their mental strength. The truth above all, just as Mandy Hale said, "Growth is painful. Change is painful. But nothing is as painful as staying stuck somewhere you don't belong." This is why we need to read insightful books which are a great way to invest in our personal development. This enables us to take our life and business up to the next level mostly with books that focus on leadership, philosophy, finances, problem solving and strategy.

Be Bold And Face Your Fears

"Nothing in life is to be feared, it is only to be understood. Now is the time to understand more, so that we may fear less".
Marie Curie

According to one-time American activist Rosa Parks, *"I have learned over the years that when one's mind is made up, this diminishes fear; knowing what must be done does away with fear".* April 6, 2014, was a remarkable day in the history of the wrestling world event tagged WrestleMania 30 which was staged by The Undertaker and Brock Lesnar. After a serious beating recorded on both sides, Brock Lesnar was able to defeat the undefeated streak which really shocked the world of wrestling as a whole. The fact is, Brock Lesnar was able to do the impossible because he was bold enough to face his fears. While in the ring, Brock Lesnar had the choice of giving up the fight because it wasn't an easy one at any point of the match. But commonly said, he who runs from fighting would live to fight another day. In a few words, Brock Lesnar, later became the WWE World Heavyweight Champion. From the scenario, each time Brock Lesnar was beaten, he bears the pains and carries on by fighting back for his dream. Dale Carnegie once said, *"if you want to conquer fear, don't sit home and think about it, go out and get busy".* Fear is just an imaginary platform to get us backwards or make us give up at the point of winning. The point is, we have the choice to either fight back for our desired life or let it be lived by someone else. Fear disallows us from doing the needful at the right time and makes us regret missed opportunities that would have transformed our lives for the better. When we allow fear into our lives, it becomes easier for circumstances to determine the extent at which we could go in life and also disallows us from fully actualizing our potential.

According to Eleanor Roosevelt, the former American political figure, "you gain strength, courage, and confidence by every experience in which you really stop to look fear in the face. You are able to say to yourself, 'I lived through this horror. I can take the next thing that comes along". The fact is, no matter where we are currently, we can take a step forward but if we allow fear, would we see the light at the end of the tunnel which later becomes a sufficient reason to back out or give up. Without any form of doubt, taking one little step forward makes us a better version than our previous state. The so-called fear has deprived many of taking reasonable risks and having full control of their lives' by replacing actions with excuses and great achievements with sentiments. Truth be told, greater accomplishments are for those who are realistic and persistent in their reasonable causes in a fearless manner. Fear facilitates self-doubts which in turn leads to inaction and later limitations and regrets.

According to Jim Morrison, the American singer and songwriter, "expose yourself to your deepest fear; after that, fear has no power, and the fear of freedom shrinks and vanishes, you are free". Having the courage to face our fears in life changes our story for the better and also enables us to create a positive impact in the lives of others, however, being fearless enables our voice to be discovered by the right people for us. Novelist Paulo Coelho once said, "here is only one thing that makes a dream impossible to achieve: the fear of failure". In life, the fear of failure makes one a coward and according to William Shakespeare, "A coward dies a thousand times before his death". The fact is, negative imagination such as 'I am not that good enough' or 'I am unsuitable for purpose', is the main cause of fear, followed by reflection from past mistakes either ours or that of others around us. Back to the scenario of the wrestling ring, the place of no play or pretence but for the fittest and serious minded. It takes persistent efforts to weaken one's opponent while in the ring and also preserving all kinds of punches before the winner could be declared. In many cases, the loser might decide to challenge the winner another day after he might have learnt from what really caused the failure. The fact is, losing in any situation is never the end of the world as some outcomes we face in life might be situational and not a real reflection of who we are. Therefore, we should not see any good reason why we shouldn't try again. According to Jack Hyles, "Success is on the same road as failure; success is just a little further down the road". In a few words, those who try to make mistakes or fail are far better than those who did nothing simply because of fear. One point I would like to stress on is that fearful thoughts are designed to keep us safe and limited. They are not wisdom, and they are not the truth. We need to choose what we want in life.

Rather than allowing fear to determine our choice in life, it's better we learn how best to handle it. One thing we don't understand is that it's impossible to think clearly when we're flooded with fear or anxiety. The first thing to do is to take time out so we can physically calm down. Another fact is, avoiding failure as a result of fear only makes it scarier but studying the situation in a critical manner reduces the level of fear within us and when we begin to make moves, the fear will fade away with time. When battling with fear or doubts, it is paramount to think of the regrets attached to ditching the envisioned goal which could change our lives around for the best. Another way of overcoming fear is by sharing it with others to avoid being frustrated on any issue. Sharing fears with others should facilitate the development of an imaginary or possible solution, it also includes working hard on our personal development to enlighten us more about life as a whole.

Furthermore, overcoming fear might require going back to basics or the drawing board which might help in getting a clear view or in-depth analysis of the situation to be approached. As commonly said, a problem well understood is half solved, it becomes easier to devise the rightful strategies to deal with the main cause of fear. In today's world professionals such as public speakers and musicians would need to learn how to overcome the fear of facing a huge crowd, without that, their voices can never be heard. By and large, the main aim of fear is to limit us on the long run in terms of fulfilling our potentials and living our dreams but it's up to us to allow it or face it down because it's our responsibility to make a choice.

To clear the air, fear, weakness and defeat dwell in the mind and there are the biggest psychological robbers of one's destiny as what they all do is to facilitate inaction. According to one of the former African military heads of state. The fear of war made his childhood stay from the initial training back in the early 70's. The fear emerged from the postal and the words of the training officers. After years of joining the military, he was sent on various professional courses both local and international towards having a progressive career which led him to the rank of a general. In light of a military coup, he was made to head the nation because he was the most senior officer in the army back then. So likewise, in life, any situation we give up is always an edge for someone else and it is also a reflection that we are unprepared and unfit for the task. My advice at this junction is that we might come across numerous defeats in life but we shouldn't be defeated. And bear this in mind, being determined and focused are the major platforms to overturn tough situations in life to a bearable one. I would like to share the life story of Jennifer Hudson, the popular American singer. She had the passion for music from childhood which boosted her confidence and entered for the American idol competitions. The audition process created a huge fear in her as she was nervous but she went ahead and performed on stage. After performing brilliantly on stage, the judges and fans were amazed by her talent which made her an early favourite. She was voted off mid-way through the season and came 7th.

GET IT RIGHT YOUR CHOICE IS YOUR DESTINY

That didn't stop her from pursuing her dream, as she was later invited to a movie audition and outperformed many professional singers and actors. In a few words, she won an academy award for her first movie role. She made it clearly in her appreciation speech that she couldn't believe she could make until she gave it a try. Not the end, she later won a Grammy award for her album Jennifer Hudson in 2009. Despite the occurrence of the unthinkable and unexpected while she was on a musical tour, she still made it back to public life after the whole grief and shock. Meaning, no matter how negative our life might be at any point, we should still try our best to look for the positive situation. We never know how strong we are until we overcome tough times in life. And being bold to face down our fears in life disallow tragedies to define us and also disallow fear from blocking or limiting our potentials in life. By and large, Jennifer Hudson, once at some point, we have the power to choose how we are going to handle every situation we are faced with throughout our lives. In other words, if we can't face down our fears and challenges, we should forget about being successful in life.

Above all, there are two sides of fear in life, we either forget everything and run meaning burying our vision or face everything it requires and rise beyond expectation and doubts of others. However, the choice is ours. When you see a successful person, do not judge him or her by the fruits of success that he is tasting today, but you must be able to understand that it is all about the years of effort that could finally lead him to what he has achieved today. Attaining a fulfilled life is never a day job or any form of magic, Successful people have a lot of struggle behind their success which gets covered in the limelight. Every successful person, be it famous people like Albert Einstein, Thomas Edison, the Wright Brothers or a small farmer or a businessman all underwent sheer hard work and various recorded failures to reach where they stand today. Above all, we are what we see of ourselves and not the imagination of others. Just as stated by Amanda Gorman in her Inaugural Poem: For there is always light, if only we're brave enough to see it. If only we're brave enough to do it. The simple truth is, those we celebrate today are those who stood yesterday by doing something specific for themselves and valuable to others.

Live In The Present

"If you want to be happy, do not dwell in the past, do not worry about the future, focus on living fully in the present."
Roy T. Bennett, The Light in the Heart

Apart from being enlightened in life which enables us to grow both philosophically and psychologically with the ability to think critically before choosing whatever course we stand for in life. We need to learn to live in the present moment of our lives, to make the very possible best of our time and dwell in a state of readiness for the future. Living in the present enables us to draw accurate insight from our past regardless of how lovely or funny it might be, making use of those insights serving as lessons for today and a platform for a brighter future. It gives a clue of a reasonable solution for whatever challenges we might have been battling with such as fear, limitations or negative emotions to avoid us from getting stuck to our past. It's better to fail and move on with the flow, than be successful and remain at the same point. However, moving on with flow increases our chances of getting help, support or making adjustments rather than remaining at the same point which is a receipt towards giving up. According to Earl Nightingale, "*Learn to enjoy every minute of your life. Be happy now. Don't wait for something outside of yourself to make you happy in the future. Think how precious the time you have to spend, whether it's at work or with your family. Every minute should be enjoyed and savoured*". To justify this quote, Zig Ziglar once said, "*the past is your lesson,*

LIVE IN THE PRESENT

the present is your gift, the future is your motivation i.e. the cause which inspires us for the best and not joining the rest".

The more we are able to learn, the more precisely we are able to see and handle our gifts and the more we are able to utilize it for tomorrow's opportunities. Tomorrow would come with better opportunities but what we get from those opportunities is determined by how well prepared we are today. As I usually say, living in the present is a typical reflection of us being in full control of our lives by handling emotions rather than it handling us. To iron my point, mistakes and regrets are inevitable in life but our ability to turn the situation around makes us stronger and a better version of ourselves. According to Dale Carnegie, *"Develop success from failures. Discouragement and failure are two of the surest stepping stones to success"*. To place the icing on the cake, there's a common saying, *"I regret nothing in my life even if my past was full of hurt, I still look back and smile, because it made me who I am today".*

Eckhart Tolle. Once said, *"realize deeply that the present moment is all you ever have"*. No matter what we face at the moment, we should understand the fact that mistakes are inevitable and the only thing we need to concern ourselves with at the moment is bettering ourselves. Bettering ourselves would enable us to aim high and prepare for a better tomorrow. never should we be a prisoner of our own past because it was just a lesson not a life sentence, and bear in mind, falling down is an accident and staying down is a choice. Sticking to sad memories would always keep us down and take us nowhere. It's only when we train ourselves to restrain from past abuses or rejections, we are able to think rightly and focus on what we can do best to actualize our desires. The past is finite but the future is infinite. The past is a finite story book with all the chapters already completed. We cannot make the past better than it was or worse than it was. It really is what it is. The simple truth is, if we do not get rid of our past then our past will get rid of us both now and in the future. Getting stuck in the vacuum gives a limited view about the future, mostly when following leaders with myopic views, we end up regretting. However, we should never allow our errors in judgment or views to reoccur to afford us going down the wrong path. But we need to try to improve ourselves by studying the cause of errors and returning to basics with the aim of making a big difference in how we get things back on track.

Living in the present is a typical reflection which indicates the fact that we are completely aware of where we are at a particular moment of our lives or living in the happening. That is, we are centred on the here and now. Also, we are not worried about the future or thinking about the past. As Albert Einstein did say," *Life is like riding a bicycle, to keep your balance you must keep moving*". Living in the present starts from having total control over our thoughts because as a man thinketh so he is (Proverbs 23 v 7). Sara Ajna in her words said, "the sun is a daily reminder that we too can rise again from the darkness, that we too can shine our own light". In a few words, living in the past keeps us in the dark and makes us ignorant of what is ahead of us but our desire to be better than our previous state instils confidence into us to act regardless of the risks and distractions on the way or in the process. It renews our energy and boosts our ability to change things around for the best which we desire.

According to Mitch Carson, *"we aim above the mark to hit the mark"*. Aiming higher for a better tomorrow is not something of the past but a product of living in the moment. And take it or leave it, it's only crops well planted at the right time and on the right soil that grows as desired. In reality, living in the present is the major platform of turning the past impossibilities to possibilities and limitations to excellence. Without any form of pretence, the world is ever moving and living in the past or over thinking about the future rather than preparing for it are personal choices we make either because that wouldn't stop anyone from moving with the flow of change. Living in the moment includes having a better insight of what to be done now to have a better say tomorrow. We need to get it clear; life unfolds in the present and not in the past, the more we allow the present to slip off us either by indolence, distractions or ignorance, the more we end up blaming ourselves tomorrow. According to one of our childhood proverbs, what a pity, that pity couldn't pity itself at the right time, this connotes the fact that the past is gone and there's no future in it. According to Stephen Schueller, "focusing on the present moment also forces you to stop over thinking". "Being present-minded takes away some of that self-evaluation and gets lost in our mind. The fact is if we want a future with significance we need to inhabit the present by doing the needful such as investing in ourselves before having expectations for tomorrow by setting reasonable goals and backing them with action. We need to stop dwelling on past accomplishments because it would prevent us from doing more today and attain a greater tomorrow.

Living in the present gives us a greater sense of fulfilment because we won't be thinking about what we've left behind or previous mistakes but rather improving ourselves for life changing opportunities ahead of us. By learning to live in the present, we would find it easier to let go of regrets and grudges of the past and focus on what is expected of us to go the extra mile. We would have more energy to execute plans towards our desired goals. Living in the present makes us happier and more appreciative. It also makes us confident about what we working towards. Life is not all about what others think about us but understanding what we want and how to get it is what matters. Living in the present would keep us above unproductive situations such as waiting unnecessarily for inspiration instead of doing research to discover what needs to be addressed. It would also help to level ourselves above people's opinion rather than getting ourselves grounded. Nothing else would keep us focused on what is necessary at the right time other than having the ability to live in the present instead of trying to please others or trying to be perfect. It gives us the ability to be independently minded towards running our race in life rather than comparing ourselves to others to avoid being criticized. We can only avoid repeating the same mistakes always keeping us backwards or stationed by living in the present and understanding the causes of previous failures. An African proverb says, do not look where you fell but why you slipped.

One of the better ways we can live the present moments of our lives, while working and hoping for a better tomorrow is learning from the past errors (either ours or others) and applying the right principles. Elon Musk is a typical example of someone who lives in the present moment because he worked hard to bring imaginations to reality. According to him, anyone who wishes to be successful in life should be able to read often towards leading, he also said, one should take risk at the right time before life gets in the way i.e. doing the right thing at the right time. Any serious-minded person shouldn't be a trend follower but a trendsetter. In other words, to live your life, you don't need the permission of others or follow a common scheme to be fulfilled in life. To live in the present, is to live a fulfilled life and to be fulfilled, we need to find and understand the good courses in whatever choice we make in life. If not, we will find it easy to chase another man's dream ignorantly. As I usually say, where we stand determines who sees us and what we attract to our lives for the purpose of having it well tomorrow, let's start by being creative instead of complaining and also plan to be successful but be ready for failure along the journey.

To stress my point, failure is simply the opportunity to begin again, this time more intelligently and tough situations produce strong minded people. According to Tony Robbins, your freedom begins when you leave behind the bullshit story on why you don't have it. In essence, our ability to free our minds from our past mistakes, failures and setbacks is what changes our story. I do get inspired by the stories of Arnold Schwarzenegger, the actor and the Former Governor of California in the United States and Howard Schultz, the American businessman. Arnold Schwarzenegger was violently abused as a child, he struggled with relentless anxiety and barely spoke English when he moved

LIVE IN THE PRESENT

to America. The truth and nothing more is that living in the past would do us no good rather than taking us down the wrong path which would always make the past better than the future. We need to believe in ourselves and our desired life and also in the fact that the future would always be better than the past. However, it's paramount to live in the fullness of the present before being able to catch up with the greatness of tomorrow.

Living in the present is about having a compelling future of contributing value to mankind and not being a liability to others. It's having the capacity for growth, choosing to live above limits which could be determined by learning from past experiences or failures and having the ability to remain relevant and not outdated. However, no matter what challenges we face, we still need to believe in ourselves and the potential outcome of whatever we are doing at the moment which includes the choices we make, also we should believe our best moments are still ahead of us while we give in our possible best today to accomplish what others wouldn't be able to tomorrow. As we all know, the past is and would remain an experience, while the present is an experiment. However, the future is an expectation and to live our best we need to make use of experience to perform our experiment to achieve our expectations.

Stand For Something Or Fall For Anything

"When you stand for something, you've got to stand for it all the way, not half way".
Kevin Gates

It was the twenty-first birthday of a young promising lady, and the father walked up to her to ask what she would like him to buy for her as he had initially promised to buy anything she wants, once she clocks twenty-one years. After some minutes of thinking about what was good for her, she requested an expensive nice car which was the latest model as at then. The father, being a man of his words, placed an order for her dream car without any form of hesitation in her name. After so much excitement with her friends, they decided to go and paint the town red by visiting the cinema and have some eat outs. The young lady, being an experienced car owner, went ahead and drove through bus lanes during enforcement time simply because these lanes seemed to her the best alternative routes without knowing she had been caught on camera a couple of times that fateful day. Weeks after the incident occurred, she received six penalty charges notices from local traffic enforcement authority in which pictures of herself and her friends were clearly attached to the notice. Ignorance of the law remains inexcusable; a picture of the enforceable sign was placed on the notice along with the contravention code which is the statement that justifies the penalty. The young lady gradually became uncomfortable with the situation at hand as she was confused on what to do or whom to call. After several attempts to get those notifications cancelled, she was made to face more charges for losing the appeal. She later turned to the father who sat her down after paying utmost attention to her troubles. The father responded: My lovely daughter, I strongly believe you have now come of age and now need to begin to get used to the realities of life which starts by facing the challenges of whatever choice we make. I also believe you know what is good for you before you make your request and you should be able to handle whatever is yours regardless of how you got them. It was your choice to request for a car and not any other thing, it was your choice to call on friends to celebrate with you and it was your choice to drive on the bus lane while other road users were avoiding it. However, ignorance of the law is not an excuse, you had the choice to pay the fine at the initial stage before the accumulating stage and yet you still have a choice to pay off your debt now or let it have an adverse effect on your credit rating which could further deny you some other credit facilities for years. So, buying you a car doesn't mean I would also fuel it for you that's why it was registered in your name.

The bottom line of the story is that we are responsible for whatever choice we make in any aspect of life. It was clear that the young lady had been a Daddy's pet and was not used to facing such situations simply because it wasn't part of what she was taught while at school. In reality, no matter what she chooses to do after the conversation with her father, it's her choice and she only would have to face the outcome of the situation. The story of the young lady is a typical reflection of why I decided to write this book because many continuously blame their past for their current situation and still believe it's the main reflection on their future. I see this as a result of typical ignorance and loss of self-esteem. This book shares the reasons why we need to think critically to break off from any form of intellectual bondage or vacuum created by us unknowingly or by the unknown.

Taking a stand means to take a firm decision against what is wrong for us, as commonly known that a man who chooses to stand for nothing will fall for anything. In life, what we stand for defines who we are and the extent we attain. A man who can't courageously stand for whatever good course would hardly chart his course in life. After many years of relating with various kinds of people, I came to realize that the reason why many never went far in life is simply because they spent their lifetime trying to please others, trying to be like others or pretending to justify wrong causes in an intellectual manner with the aim of gaining a sense of belonging. To stand for something simply means to hold firmly to a particular opinion or belief in life wholeheartedly which enables our voice to be created and heard and also influence others positively. According to Tiffany Madison, *"If we don't fight for what we 'stand for' with our passionate words and honest actions, do we really 'stand' for anything?"*. One thing I would like to make clear is that, the past is our head and that's why we could remember it and learn from the mistakes we made but the future being our hands, we could predict it by being well prepared for it and make a positive reflection on it by drawing insights from the lesson we learn from the past. History has made many people famous just because of the course and believe they stood for which created a positive impact in others such as human rights movements or politics. The fact is, the world will not know you if you don't present yourself to them with significance. To stand for a reasonable course for the purpose of humanity, we need to be a true version of ourselves and be courageous enough to speak out without any form of contradiction or bias. It's a matter of standing up for our beliefs fearlessly.

According to Winston Churchill, *"Courage is what it takes to stand up and speak; courage is also what it takes to sit down and listen"*. In real terms, either to stand for something significant and specific in life or stand back and become a victim of circumstances are choices we either make. Standing for something is more sacrificing than our personal interest. Martin Luther King Jr, once said, *"A man who won't die for something is not fit to live"*. History would never erase the positive impact of Mary Mitchell Slessor, the Scottish Presbyterian missionary to Nigeria, who stopped the killing of twins and the introduction of Christianity in Nigeria back in the early nineteenth century. Today, her belief and effort had a huge significance in people's life. According to Edmund Burke, *"The only thing necessary for the triumph of evil is for good men to do nothing"*. In a few words, if we don't stand for a reasonable cause in the time of need, things might go from frying pan to fire and the required change would never be a reality.

Mother Teresa once said in her lifetime, *"I am not sure exactly what heaven will be like, but I know that when we die and it comes to time for God to judge us, he will not ask, " How many good things have you done in your life? rather he will ask, How much love did you put into what you did?"*. Drawing inspiration from this quote which is a typical reflection of which Mother Teresa stands for. She was a great follower of humanity. Mohandas Karamchand Gandhi, the Indian activist would never be forgotten for his great effort in role in securing Indian independence and how he inspired movements for civil rights and freedom across the world. He stood for a course that the world enjoys today. We are what we believe, our belief triggers our action, we are well known and responsible for our actions which is a typical reflection of who we are and who we are likely to be if entrusted in future. Of course, we choose whatever we want in life but the fact is, do we act or stand based on what we desire for the future? In today's charismatic world, people silence their opinions and lose their authenticity in an attempt to be liked by everyone or to appease both sides of an ideological division regarding it as maturity. The truth is, such people lack the understanding of standing for something or falling for nothing. Some would act on pretence with the motive of covering their confusion or ignorance. In reality, standing up for a belief where breaking new grounds might be tough and an uncomfortable decision to make but the reward would be impactful and positive in the long run. Choosing not to stand for a right cause at the time would only enable one to lose its own identity, freedom and also damage potential opportunities. Rather, it would be wise of us to pursue the course we believe to be the right one and avoid being a faceless body in the crowd. It's wise to choose freedom in any situation and becoming an authentic version of oneself. According to Will Smith, *"don't chase people, be yourself, do your own thing and work hard, the right people are the ones who really belong in your life will come and stay"*. With such a belief, one would be able to identify the best people to associate with and not force friendship on others.

Henry Ford, the founder of Ford motors, once said, *"my best friend is the one who brings out the best in me"*. Not pretending in abundance and few in scarcity. According to Shannon L. Alder, *"it is better to be alone than to become a person that loses his soul to the fear of loneliness"*. Standing alone reflects how strong we are and allows us to think positive about ourselves and discover more in terms of what we are capable of achieving in life. Standing for something in life requires believing in ooneself and trying to improve from where we are currently and not camouflaging. Also practicing what we believe and stand for in a consistent manner. Saying this now and that later or acting differently from one's words would avoid other people taking us seriously or as an incompetent person to be followed or entrusted. We need to be convicted and understand the cause we stand for in life to avoid confusion and contradictions which might reflect us as one with unstable character. We need to have a deep insight into what supports or opposes our belief and develop the passion for the same cause to avoid it being faded. According to William Ernest Henley, in his poem titled Invictus, *"In the fell clutch of circumstance, I have not winced nor cried aloud. Under the bludgeoning of chance my head is bloody, but unbowed"*. Meaning, the more pains it takes to stand for whatever we believe in life, the more we should cherish it and the more we should refuse to give up. It's our responsibility to admire whatever we love and wish to see while remaining inexcusable regardless of the pains, obstacles and let down that comes our way.

Our choice of standing up and fighting for our distinguished course today will reflect on our uniqueness tomorrow, while understanding the principle of 'here today, there tomorrow' and not any form of magic. A lot of people became celebrities and ambassadors of multinational organisations because they stood and voiced out for the vulnerable to be protected within the society and many do by giving to good courses in which later bless them in return one way or the other. What we stand for reflects our values, drives our words and actions. Standing for something is an indication of having one's future ahead and not behind which enables us to become an achiever and not a deceiver. Abbe Pierre would never be forgotten in history for his humanitarian work in setting up a charity for the homeless. Also, Malala Yousafzai, the Pakistani schoolgirl who defied threats of the Taliban to campaign for the right to education. She survived being shot in the head by the Taliban and has become a global advocate for human rights, women's rights and the right to education. What we stand for in life answers questions such as What am I passionate about? and What are my core values in life? Freedom was what mattered to Harriet Tubman when she escaped from slavery and later helped lead slaves to freedom. She also served as agent and leader during the civil war and later became a symbol of the slavery abolition movement. It's tough standing out when many are aiming to fit in or belong to a cause that would never benefit them in the long run, it's about having the right sense and intention of getting the right thing done for the sake of humanity and not selfish reasons. It's about operating with faith over fear, courage over self-doubt or regardless of what others might think, it keeps us going and keeps us growing.

GET IT RIGHT YOUR CHOICE IS YOUR DESTINY

However, when we decide to stand and fight a specific course in life, we should avoid unreasonable compromise by focusing more on the potential impact to be created rather than the current pains and challenges we are faced with. To clear the air, if we focus on the hurt, we will continue to suffer and get frustrated in the long run but if we focus on the lesson, the more insightful we become and grow towards becoming a better version of ourselves. At times, we might feel lonely and insecure while standing out for a genuine purpose but it's better being a lonely lion than a popular sheep. That's why we need to understand the fact that while fighting for a course we should never feel defeated or humiliated in any way because fighting a reasonable course is never the same as whipping a dead horse. As a matter of fact, while standing for a paramount course in life, either within our family or the society at large, we need to understand that we might be misunderstood for a while but knowing the impact would always be recognized for generations to come. Such were the cases of Martin Luther King Jr and Nelson Mandela, the duo stood for equality during their lifetime. Shakespeare once said, *"I always feel happy because I don't expect anything from anyone, expectations always hurt, life is short so love your life be happy and keep smiling that's life- feel it live it and enjoy it"*. But it's up to us to have a clear understanding of what bothers us in life and the genuine need to figure it out before it addresses us in a ridiculous manner. Get it right, the more we expect from others, the more we expose ourselves to frustration and intimidation, however, expecting unnecessarily instead of working out alternatives reflects that we are not fully determined about what we intend to achieve or what we stand for in life. Brian Tracy, the popular motivational speaker, did hammer on this point in one of his quotes, *"Peak performance begins with you taking complete responsibility for your life and everything that happens to you.*

According to Dwayne Johnson, also known as 'The rock', *"hard work beats talent"*. Doing a critical study about the semi-retired professional wrestler and American actor, hard work has been what he stands for and believes. He recorded a good number of successes in various endeavours such as college football, professional wrestling and acting. He believes in understanding what he wants, how to get it done without any form of excuses and taking action. His philosophy is sufficient to make him break limits and stand out for significance without any form of sentiment. Our philosophy enables us to think both tactically and strategically and also makes us progressive. Our ability to think enables us to see beyond challenges but the value in our chosen course. Bear in mind, significance is attained by doing the hard work while others are busy wishing for it. Our ability to stand for something in life makes us an example to others because we help to realize that failure is part of any successful process and it's always temporary in nature. They come to realize at some point their discovered potentials and later attain something greater than themselves. Just as Winston Churchill, the former British prime minister once said, *"success is moving from failure to failure with enthusiasm"*. When we stand for a course, we help others build and develop a positive attitude which is required for a successful life. By and large, it's essential for us to be diligent by standing for what we believe and avoid judging ourselves by the standard of others i.e. a copycat. It's clear that we've all gotten different goals in life, just as that of a chef and a boxer and our means of attaining them differs. Rohit Adlakha once said, *"the sea is common for all, but some take pearls, some fish and some come out with just wet legs"*. Like the world is the same and common to all, yet we get what we try for. And to crown it up, John D. Rockefeller, the American business magnate said, *"Don't be afraid to give up the good to go for the great"*.

Getting Rid Of Negative Voices

"Don't focus on negative things; focus on the positive, and you will flourish".
Alek Wek

A group of frogs were travelling through the woods, and two of them fell into a deep pit. When the other frogs saw how deep the pit was, they told the two frogs that they were as good as dead. The two frogs ignored the comments and tried to jump up out of the pit with all their might. The other frogs kept telling them to stop, that they were as good as dead. Finally, one of the frogs took heed to what the other frogs were saying and gave up and remained in the pit.

The other frog continued to jump as hard as he could. Once again, the crowd of frogs yelled at him to stop the pain and just die. He jumped even harder and finally made it out. When he got out, the other frogs said, "Did you not hear us?" The frog explained to them that he was deaf. He thought they were encouraging him the entire time.

Taking a philosophically view of the short and inspirational story, both frogs were faced with the same challenge but had different perspectives regarding the situation which was reflected in the choice they made. The frog which gave in, in the pit might have gotten plans for the future but as far he remains in the pit, his vision or plans remain tattered. The clever frog never made it by magic, but having the right determination and taking the right action at the right time. Moreover, the clever frog was able to get rid of the negative voices from the other frogs by taking their awful advice in a positive way and gain more strength while the unproductive frog allowed the opinion of other frogs to shape its reality. As Joel Osteen once said "you cannot hang out with negative people and expect to live a positive life".

So likewise, when we pray or hope to be successful in life, we have the choice to either give what it takes or sit on the fence and remain comfortable like others. We have the choice to prove those negative voices wrong or justify them by either taking action which might be risky or stressful in most cases or do nothing which is absolutely convenient while hoping for a pie in the sky. Emphasizing on the need to try and not give in to those negative voices. J.K. Rowling, made it clear in one of her quotes, that "Failure is not fun, It can be awful". But living so cautiously that you never fail is worse. For the purpose of reality check, whatever would distinguish a man would facilitate discouragement and lack of support in most cases but it's up to us to make a choice. The reality is, not all dreams become reality and not all contenders in a race make it to the end. The fact is, most people fail in life or give up on their vision because they give attention to negative people and their terrible experiences rather than learning from those experiences by taking note of what needs to be taken care of before it gets rid of them like others. From my experience, negative people are perfect at imposing fear, impossibilities, setbacks and breakdown, just for the purpose of being like them.

Tommy Lasord, the former American baseball manager, opined that "the difference between the impossible and the possible lies in a person's determination". Rather than working it out and becoming successful, many prefer to fake it or live a bogus life at the advice of the negative ones who believe in criticizing success due to its risk taking or other tougher requirements. However, we shouldn't be afraid to cut negative people from our lives because they end up causing us more harm than good. Another fact is, while trying to solve problems, negative people will always come up with a reason it won't work or the need to allow the situation to have its way. One thing I would like to emphasize here is that challenges are inevitable and tough in most cases but rather than giving up, we should understand that even the tortoise can finish a race as long as he never gives up, and also believe that we can also achieve whatever our mind can conceive.

Negative people drain energy, hopes, aspirations and life out of anyone that allows them. The frog in the pit would have tried and might eventually make it but listening to negative voices made an impossible task to be accomplished. The frog was unable to think of a solution but rather took to their ill advice. At times, negative people make us feel guilty doing the needful or taking the right steps. The fact remains that, there's no way one can please negative people, they would eventually hate you simply because you refuse to be like them. According to George Bernard Shaw, "Never wrestle with a pig, you both get dirty and the pig Likes It". In reality, there's no point wasting your time with those who have nothing to offer you. Even when you're trying to help a negatively minded person you can't win because they are specialists at affecting one's attitude, discouraging one's effort, dragging one down with them to remain stagnant and see things like themselves by affecting one's thinking. As Robert Tew once said, "Don't let negative and toxic people rent space in your head. Raise the rent and kick them out and if they thrive on attention, don't give them". it's not by force others must have the same vision with you or understand your vision.

The truth is that for us to live our very best, we need to know and understand both our purpose and passion in life, surround ourselves with people who are constantly looking forward to improving themselves and desire to help discover more of ourselves by setting high and reasonable goals. Also help with various possible approaches to achieving those goals. Negative people will simply reinforce anything negative that you say, and give you all the reasons why you're right in your negativity and toxic thinking. Positive people will tell you, you can do it, and will give you positive reinforcement which is what you need when you have doubts. Michael Bassey Johnson, once said "Believing in negative thoughts is the single greatest obstruction to success". The fact is, to live a successful life and actualize our dreams we need to excuse ourselves from shallow and callous minded individuals, that is, those who have solutions to every problem. The issue is, the use of our mind either makes one successful or a failure because mind-set is what separates the best from the rest and that's why we should never allow past experiences or that of others to paralyse us from seeing the way forward or becoming a yardstick for the future.

At times, we make wrong choices simply because we want to belong to a group of associates, try not to feel guilty of others or want to keep relationships with some others. The truth according to Will Smith, "don't chase people, be yourself, do your own thing and work hard". The right people, that is, the ones who really belong in your life will come to you and stay. To be factual, negative people will make you believe your doubts and make you lock yourself up in your comfort zone mostly when with a weak determination, while positive people will motivate and convince you of your current skill and make you a better version of yourself. Positive people would make you believe in yourself which is the first secret to success. They inspire the required confidence to make you believe in yourself and act and transform your life. They assist you to determine your goals, learn how to achieve it through effective planning. One thing we need to understand is that our level of success is only predetermined by our level of effort and that's why we need to surround ourselves with people who got insight to help us aim higher and not the myopic ones who only drive us crazy by making our ideas and opinions look stupid and also dispose your dreams. In short, it's worthwhile staying away from negative people so as to bring out the best in us.

To place the icing on the cake, never allow yourself to be limited by other people's limited imagination because what you see or create is what you get. Another point is, every mistake should be taken as a platform for learning and not establishing failure. According to Denis Waitley, "Failure should be our teacher, not our undertaker, failure is delay, not defeat". It is a temporary detour, not a dead end. Failure is something we can afford to do or determine our lifestyle only by saying nothing, doing nothing, and being nothing. That's why you need to create a great future with your imagination. However, your doubts create mountains while your actions move them. Above all, people might quit for whatever reason but the most important thing is we should never quit ourselves. Also, all we need is to possess the ability to be resilient to enable us to adapt to tough situations and bounce back regardless of the negativities we face. Mark Twain, the American writer, "Keep away from those who try to belittle your ambitions". Small people always do that, but the real great people make you believe that you too can become great.

Stay Connected To Your Goals

"There are no secrets to success. It is the result of preparation, hard work, and learning from failure".
Colin Powell

The best way to live our lives is by taking our destiny into our hands and whether we like it or not, our perception is our reality. Apart from having an idea of whatever we want to be or achieve in life and how to achieve those goals. Making our vision a reality is another important choice we need to make in life. According to Napoleon Hill, *"when your desires are strong enough, you will appear to possess superhuman powers to achieve"*. No matter what we face in life, there's no point in pocketing or burying our ambition for the sake of fear, pleasing others or whatever reason. According to Paulo Coelho, the Brazilian lyricist and novelist, *"there is only one thing that makes a dream impossible to achieve: the fear of failure"*. People might not see the reality in your vision or dreams or invest in your ideas simply because it's not common or tangible. It's up to you to work it out regardless of what it takes. The fact is, challenges prepare the serious minded for greater heights in life at some point. Life is all about making choices. Always do your best to make the right ones and always do your best to learn from the wrong ones. No one can force growth in anyone because it's a personal choice and no matter how we get motivated, no one can force us to act. We are a product of our choices. In fact, do whatever it takes to accomplish your goals. Work hard, work smart, and put in hard work every single day to be the best version of yourself as much as possible. According to the English actor, Idris Elba, *"I've always had ambition, and the acting was successful and put my name on the map, but it was never the plan to stop there"*.

When our progress and ambition make others see us as a threat, the best thing to do is to develop ourselves towards becoming an opportunity and not a liability to ourselves and others. If we are progressive minded, we would come to realize that the level we attain in life has its own different dose of challenges. However, each dose we come across at various levels requires different momentum to overcome and that's why we need to be more committed and focused towards achieving our goals and not depending on previous strength. Elon Musk once said, *"It is possible for ordinary people to choose to be extraordinary"*. In reality, this could be possible if we are determined and action-oriented. In leadership, apart from honesty and integrity, commitment to presumed goals is another essential quality expected of any leader because once commitment is lost, carrying others along becomes boring and expectations become unattainable. To go the extra mile in life, you need to be keen in knowing what your next steps are in which should be clearly stated and understood. This facilitates making an applicable plan, idea generation and a clear map for the future. Bear in mind, your ignorance is your fault and your plans are your guide and blue print.

Pele once said, "Success is no accident. It is hard work, perseverance, learning, studying, sacrifice and most of all, love what you are doing or learning to do". Personally, I am a big dreamer and planner, when passing through tough times I do tell myself I am going through this to break through and not to remain here. I do remember a particular school song which boosts the level of my confidence: *"We are going, heaven knows that we are going, we know we are: we will get there, heaven knows that we will get there, we know we will."* As a matter of fact, I never considered giving up as an option or making plans towards such but rather I might change course/plan for another time or seek alternative if situations get beyond my control and give all it takes to achieve my goal. I also love meditating on a particular song: I am a victory all the time, I am a success not a failure, I am a winner not a loser, I am the head and never the tail. Above all, Andrea Dykstra said, "in order to love who you are, you cannot hate the experiences that shaped you". This is simply because lessons learnt from life itself makes us wiser more often. Bob Proctor once said, "your purpose explains what you are doing with your life. Your vision explains how you are living your purpose. Your goals enable you to realize your vision".

People do discourage others from going the extra mile or doing the needful at the right time because they see them as threats to their personality. However, it's our responsibility to make right choices that suit our life without allowing those with myopic mind-set or short-sighted minds to impose their wishes on us because we alone account for our success and failure in life at the end of it. Bear in mind, if we are not a threat then we are prey in the hands of our users. I have come to realize apart from inactivity, most people fail in life due to lack of insight which makes them criticize the aspirations of others based on their personal outcomes, experiences and understanding of life. Many make decisions out of sentiments to please people by ignoring reality for personalities. The truth is, life has a different meaning to everyone and you are the best person to understand your life, you only need the reasonable few to help you rise and progress and not the unproductive multiple which only facilitates confusion and stagnation. The fact is, people can't help you progress beyond their current level, this is not a matter of love or hate and that's why we need to learn from those ahead of us and keep our aspirations real in order to achieve our numerous goals.

One day you will be exactly where you want to be, until then, keep going, keep believing, keep learning, keep working, keep growing and keep Investing in yourself. Your decision will not only improve your life, it will improve those around you. The reality is, we would be better-off focusing on the needful in terms of putting those little efforts in a consistent manner and avoid complaining or comparing our life to others because every fruit has its season and everyone has its own breakthrough period.

Dubai would have still remained a desert as it was back in the 1960's if not for the impact of Mohammad bin Rashid, the ruler of the UAE capital city. He was determined and committed towards refacing its face to what it is today. At the moment, Dubai is one of the famous and most beautiful cities in the world in terms of higher education, health, tourism, standard of living, housing and transportation. In reality, Dubai is growing faster than any city in the world, the truth is, the ruler had a clear vision of what he wanted to achieve and he was committed towards that. He once said, "I want my people to live a better life in their country now and not twenty years". This was his main goal which fuels his actions. Taking insights from Mohammad bin Rashid mission, it is crystal clear that the only limit to our impact is our imagination and commitment towards what we want in life. The next is, we can hardly make an impact when we are unrealistic with ourselves. Above all, life has gotten nothing to offer anyone anything other than what we create for ourselves. According to Steve Maraboli, the American writer, *"While intent is the seed of manifestation, action is the water that nourishes the seed"*. Your actions must reflect your goals in order to achieve true success.

There are always insights and lessons from failures be it ours or that of others and that's why there's no point fearing taking steps. According to Muhammad Ali, *"what you are thinking is what you are becoming"*. Meaning, our imagination about ourselves and our actions determines what we become in life. As a matter of fact, we need to imagine the life we want before planning and living, it's awful living an unimaginable life and that's why we need to be insightful. Muhammad Ali, also said, *"the man who has no imagination has no wings"*. Our inability to communicate our goals and visions with the right people or like-minded does make it harder to achieve our goals in most cases. In reality, I do see people in their late fifties and early sixties pursuing a new dream rather than considering their life an error or a waste whereby many who are much younger conclude their life simply because some wrong people made them do so. The truth is, no matter your age or status, the most dangerous thing in life is to live without a vision. Many with great visions are unable to accomplish them simply because they kept awaiting the all readymade situations that is, the right time before making moves rather than building from scratch. Visionws are sure of attainment when taken from the foundation because making adjustments or corrections becomes easier and to nail it, Lionel Messi, the Argentine professional footballer opined that, "You have to fight to reach your dream". You have to sacrifice and work hard for it. This is the gospel truth and nothing more.

Truth above all, we are the product of our previous choices and it is our responsibility to ensure that our past mistakes does not determine our future positioning but we rather learn from those past experiences. Hanging out with those who have nothing to lose, making our excuses reasonable and tenderable or playing the victim to gain undue advantages would get us nowhere in life and cause us to remain the same. But if we choose to change the paradigm like {having a daily plan, setting reasonable deadlines, limiting distraction and excuses}, avoiding self-doubts such as {negative thinking and self-talk} would enable us stay authentic to ourselves and develop our philosophy with the aim of increasing our worth because knowledge is power. Reading and listening to valuable motivational materials would help us stay teachable and overcome the fear of failure, procrastination, becoming more resourceful, and asking the right questions at the right time to make life more meaningful.

To place the icing on the cake, the former Israeli Prime Minister, Golda Meir, once said, *"Make the most of yourself by fanning the tiny, inner sparks of possibility into flames of achievement"*. You don't need to start big, just as Pablo Picasso, did make it clear, *"Set small goals for yourself and meet them. You are responsible to take care of yourself. You should be your priority. Our goals can only be reached through a vehicle of a plan, in which we must fervently believe, and upon which we must vigorously act. There is no other route to success"*. Truth be told, if you want to transform your life, you need to learn how to set goals, so you can design your own future. Above all, Michael Jordan once said *"You must expect great things from yourself before you can do them"*.

Learn From All Mistakes

"Our greatest glory is not in never falling, but in getting up every time we do".
Confucius

Many years ago, there lived a young and ambitious man who struggled to create a beautiful trademark suitable for clothing and other items. Due to the lack of funds to actualize his dream, he was advised to contact a well-known cloth merchant who had produced a number of designer wears on a large scale aiming to be sold over the next few years and earning a fortune. Having understood the negative impact of the young man's beautiful trade mark on his business, the merchant at first asked if the trade mark was registered and offered the young man some money for lunch. The merchant later invited him to a dinner where he was able to make enticing promises if the young man would agree to partner with him. He made up false stories of people who had partnered and prospered with him in the past and the young man began to see himself living his luxurious dream not knowing it was a pie in the sky. Cutting the long story short, out of excitement the young man signed an agreement with the merchant which disallowed him presenting or producing the trade mark with anyone else for the next ten years. His inability to read within the lines got him trapped for ten years. And not only that, his major mistakes were, he never understood the value and the potential impact of his trademark in which the merchant does, he was seeking for partnership with a lovely rival dominating the market and his lack of wisdom made him sell his birthright for a plate of pottage. I know the young man would learn from his mistake as it is up to us to conduct a reality check on ourselves and to identify where reasonable adjustments are required before others begin to take advantage of us through underestimating us and leading us astray. One thing we should realize is that rivals exist everywhere and they are no jokers, this is why we need to be the best player of our own destiny.

As generally believed, life is said to be a journey, however, the hidden and golden truth is, life is a distance to some and a stone throw to many. Either a journey, a distance or a stone throw, life is whatever we make out of it. The fact is, when a man considers life as a journey and hangs out with those who take life as a distance or as a stone throw, he is bound to ruin his dream, lose focus and struggle unnecessarily. According to Andy Andrews, "Life itself is a privilege, but to live life to the fullest- well, that is a choice". In reality, learning from our mistakes and turning them to stepping stones or making them a life sentence to lock us in comfort zones are choices we make either. As we grow as humans, we need to understand the need to embrace transformation rather than institutionalization is one of the best we would ever make in life. Institutionalization would only make us comfortable in a stagnant position while transformation would keep us growing, enable us to overturn challenges and prepare us for opportunities ahead of us. Replacing sentiments with reality, the way we see life reflects a lot in terms of what we are on track of becoming. Zig Ziglar once said, "when you focus on problems, you get more problems. When you focus on possibilities, you have more opportunities". Once again, life is a journey and never a straight-line graph, you are the best person to understand your journey and you own no one's explanation about it. It's up to you to find your own path which differs from others rather than taking your current situation as your final destination. According to Napoleon Hill, "You are the master of your destiny. You can influence, direct and control your own environment. You can make your life what you want it to be".

In the cause of writing this particular chapter, I made an unreversible mistake. While typing the script, I forgot to save the document before the expiration time at the local library. After so much effort to recover the document to no avail, I thought of various options such as deleting the whole chapter or rewriting it but the truth is, this book might be meaningless without this chapter or this chapter might end up as the lifter of this book. Of course, two choices were before me to take one, if I choose to delete the whole chapter, it shows I haven't learned from my mistake and I would have no experience sharing the need to be more conscious in whatever we do. I choose to do more research and rewrite it which means in life, regardless of failures, setbacks and disappointments and unexpected challenges we come across, we should always consider re-emerging rather than giving up as it is often said, resilience would always break resistance. Michael Jordan once said, "Obstacles don't have to stop you. If you run into a wall, don't turn around and give up. Figure out how to climb it, go through it, or work around it". I have come to realize as a life coach that most mistakes we make as humans were influenced by those who lack the intellectual capacity to understand our idea or vision but rather are pleased in underestimating us to consider ourselves unfit. These are those with low ambition and have nothing to offer or lose. Either we choose to achieve our dream or abandon it.

The truth is, mistakes are for personal improvements but it depends on our ability to take insight from the occurrence or carry on expressing regrets. Bear in mind, mistakes have gotten no master, but they lead to experience which facilitates personal growth and insight to handle challenges and enable us to make better choices when next possible. I'm sure if the young man had another opportunity to partner with anyone, he would be smarter than ever based on his experience with the clothing merchant. According to John C. Maxwell, "every successful person is someone who failed, yet never regarded himself as a failure".

And this is why we need to stop underestimating ourselves but find ways to grow. According to Michael Jordan, "I've missed more than 9000 shots in my career. I've lost almost 300 games. 26 times, I've been trusted to take the game winning shot and missed. I've failed over and over and over again in my life. And that is why I succeed". Truth to be told, that's the secret and nothing more.

One positive thing about making mistakes in life is that it makes us more intelligent, reasonable and creative. We get to understand more of ourselves, our dreams and strategies towards achieving our goals. The 32nd U.S. President Franklin D. Roosevelt made it clear in one of his remarkable speeches, "the only man who makes no mistakes is the man who never does anything". As I usually say, failure is never a final destination except we make it be, it's only a temporary checking point to discover what could be done better and carry on and become unstoppable. By and large, people who learn from mistakes can never get stagnated in life; rather they challenge themselves by seeking real alternative measures for advancement. Another common mistake we make is that we pay so much attention and expect so much from those who have nothing to offer themselves talk less of others and leave ourselves for those set of people to recreate us, we love to please those who aren't what they claim to be that is, a beautiful container with a poor content. John C. Maxwell said, "If you know who you are, make the changes you must in order to learn and grow, and then give everything you've got to your dreams, you can achieve anything your heart desires". Lewis Howes did mention, "Strength comes from struggle. When you learn to see your struggles as opportunities to become stronger, better, wiser, then your thinking shifts from 'I can't do this' to 'I must do this. I have learned that champions aren't just born; champions can be made when they embrace and commit to life-changing positive habits".

A young lady was given a golden necklace by her mother just to know its current value. The young lady went to the seconded Sunday market whereby she found only those who were ready to get it off her at an auction by taking it down as an old-fashioned material and can't get a better offer than they could give. She then left for a jewellery dealer who understands the value of the same old-fashioned necklace and was ready to pay a reasonable price. On getting home, she shared her experience with her mother who told that the mistake most people make in life is they position their values at the wrong place. What created a difference in the scenario was that the lady never accepted the limit placed on the jewellery but sought for the right place. The truth is still the truth; a lie is still a lie; no matter who believes it. Life is very similar to a boxing ring, defeat is not declared when we are down, it's only declared when we refuse to rise up.

Apart from understanding our ambition or the path we choose to follow in life, it's worthwhile to do more research to have a deep insight to make us more of what we could become. Our choice to dig deep in our respective field is what distinguishes us or make life more meaningful rather than being boring to ourselves because life is whatever we make it to be and we are to create whatever we want from it either for ourselves or others. Hans F Hansen once said, "it takes nothing to join the crowd but It takes everything to stand alone". Most cases when faced with challenging situations we need to be on the offensive side and not wait for the situation to have its cause before thinking of what to do. Unexpected situations are best handled when effectively prepared for it by acquiring unlimited insights from various good sources.

The little things we do and steps we take helps us achieve and protect both the little and great things we desire in life. Most people make mistakes reflecting their real value as a result of self-misunderstanding, doubts and underestimation. Dwayne Johnson, the former wrestler and actor once said, "we do today what they won't, so tomorrow we accomplish what they can't" and this is the major game changer. The truth is, making a big life change is scary. But, know what's even scarier and regrettable. Apart from learning from mistakes either ours or from others, we need to exercise our willpower to change our life to whatever we want it to be. We don't have to keep doing what we've been doing if it's not yielding the benefits we want. Also, avoid punishing yourselves for your own mistakes. According to Karon Waddell, "don't carry your mistakes around with you, place them on the floor and use them as stepping stones to where you want to go". And she also said, "Don't let people who don't care about you manipulate your mind, feelings and emotions or control how you think about yourself". Never give that much power to them. However, taking inspiration from both quotes, we are the product of whatever we could imagine about ourselves that is, either we excel in any endeavour limitlessly or limitedly depending on how we see ourselves. Get it right, limitations live only in our minds but if we channel our imaginations in the right arena, we are bound to experience a high level of possibilities and become limitless. We might need to go the extra mile than others or sharpen things to suit our desire in any unpleasant situations. Michael Phelps, the American swimmer once said, "Things won't go perfect. It's all about how you adapt from those things and learn from mistakes".

Separating sentiments from realities, the fact that you love people doesn't mean they won't depart from you someday for any reason. The relationship you have with yourself is the most complicated one because you can't walk away from yourself. You have to forgive every mistake and deal with every flaw. You have to find a way to love yourself even when you are disgusted with yourself. In the book, Lost & Found written by Nicole Williams, he wrote, "Every morning we get a chance to be different. A chance to change. A chance to be better. Your past is your past. Leave it there. Get on with the future part, honey".

A better understanding would enable us to derive lessons and insights from mistakes made and not allow it to limit or cripple us by remaining the same, mostly when people advise or judge

LEARN FROM ALL MISTAKES

us as a matter of the situation. Dale Carnegie, the American writer, said, "Instead of worrying about what people say of you, why not spend time trying to accomplish something they will admire". The fact is, waiting for those who are not ready to understand our vision, support our dreams and add value to our lives is like expecting an elephant to fly like an eagle. We could accomplish something bigger than ourselves if we can learn by searching for the missing points from the situation and possible remedies to challenges rather than giving up. According to Tony Robbins, setting goals is the first step in turning the invisible into the visible. To place the icing on the cake, learning from mistakes makes us humbler and cleverer than ever. And the ability to discipline yourself to delay gratification in the short term in order to enjoy greater rewards in the long term is the indispensable prerequisite for success. George Sheehan, the sport writer, "Success means having the courage, the determination, and the will to become the person you believe you were meant to be".

In a nutshell, we are the artiste of our lives, never should we give our paintbrush to anyone else. That's why we should stop focusing on what others are doing but learn to live our lives for ourselves which is one better platform for improvement. John C. Maxwell, wrote in his book, Good Leaders Ask Great Questions "Successful people do daily what unsuccessful people do occasionally. They practice daily disciplines. They implement systems for their personal growth and they make it a habit to maintain a positive attitude.

Keep Moving Forward

"Life is about how much you can take and keep fighting, how much you can suffer and keep moving forward".
Anderson Silva

As we continue to be a product of our choices, we would realize life is never a bed of roses, it has always been warfare in which challenges remain inevitable. Yet, we have the choice to fight on, remain at the same spot line where other unforeseen circumstances place us. The best we could do is to keep moving forward because being stagnant might be unhealthy and moving backwards might be costly. Of course, we might have to exercise patience at various points in life either after recording failure or a loss, also after winning and preparing to take on another challenge for the next level. While exercising patience, we might take the best of such an opportunity to learn something new before strategizing and later executing for a better outcome. Life is similar to finding one's self in a deep and dark valley or tunnel, regardless of what got one there or how one finds himself/herself there. The main goal is escaping out of the dark. The fact is, everything in life is attached to struggles either directly or indirectly, knowingly or unknowingly and our ability to remain persistent is what keeps us winning. For the fact things couldn't go our way doesn't mean we are failures or can't make it happen. At times, our goals or dreams do get hindered by external factors, for instance, no one ever thought of the coronavirus as at the beginning of the year 2020. However, when we find ourselves in such a situation, all we have to do is to search for alternative measures in getting things done. Bear in mind, delay doesn't mean denial. Oprah Winfrey once said, *"Challenges are gifts that force us to search for a new centre of gravity. Don't fight them. Just find a new way to stand"*.

Similar examples are football strikers and soldiers, both never fight backwards based on the cause they are trained and prepared for. Moving backward is an indication of fear and to remain standing represents the loss of ideas and confusion. In a few words, moving forward keeps us growing because it's a learning platform and a typical reflection of maturity, that is, still focusing on one's goal in a courageous manner while in pain. One of my favourite bible stories is that of Ruth and Naomi. After Naomi, Ruth and Orpah were bereaved according to the story. Naomi asked Ruth and Orpah to return home and start a new life. But Ruth made a choice to carry on with Naomi and later became blessed in the long run. The bottom line is, to keep moving, we need to understand the reason for our struggles, else it would end up being a waste of time and other resources. It's true that staying on course can be challenging when life throws unexpected punches at us but the only platform that could change one's story is keeping steadfast to oneself and keep moving. However, following the path of failures would eventually make one a typical failure, note that; failure begins when considering defeats and disappointments before an event. Whereas the simple key is that, staying positive in the midst of challenges makes us stronger and being negative makes us victims of circumstances. According to Jack Ma, the Chinese business magnate, *"never give up, today is hard, tomorrow will be worse, but the day after tomorrow will be sunshine"*. This is what we need to keep our aspirations alive. Regardless of what life tends before us as shortcuts, it would always end up in ruin.

To keep moving and winning in life, we should be ready than ever to give all it takes and never give up on our goal. Once we quit, both the goal and the trophy belong to someone else.

Another point is that goals are well achieved having a better un-derstanding of the various processes involved and not by rushing or waving magic. The fact is this, every little step results in progress which has a huge tendency of going a long way. Believe in yourself and value your goal more than the challenges surrounding it, in most cases those limit-minded and myopic relationships are the main obstacles holding us back. However, allowing them to have their way is a typical reflection of our incapability to control our lives. To carry on in life, we need to be the source of our own joy and not wait for others to give us what they don't have. To keep moving, we need to stay positive. Jenn Proske once said, *"Love yourself, It is important to stay positive because beauty comes from the inside out"*. Rather than gathering momentum and pursue that same goal once again, they consider their ages, cost to be incurred and the fear of failing again. The fact is, failing would move one forward by teaching a lesson and reflect more understanding about the cause of failure itself. Capitalizing on the fear of failure takes one no nowhere and offers nothing towards one's improvement. One thing we need to understand is that both failure and its cause are never and would never be permanent. To keep moving we need to avoid seeing life as a race or competition with others. Bear in mind, comparing one's life to that of others and allowing self-doubt are serious intellectual insults against one's personality.

In life, there are situations we can't just change, and that's the main reason we should let go of those things, not adding value to our lives. Rather, we could affect those ones within our control to our advantage. It's up to us to nurture the strength within us and get ourselves stabled to go the extra mile in life by learning to deal with disappointments and the unforeseen. Failure to handle challenges, it keeps us locked up and limited ahead of better opportunities. And when life throws us off-track, all we need to do is take time, plan effectively, refocus to gain more clarity and relaunch with a stronger mind set for peak outcome. Another fact is, we shouldn't be scared to walk alone, mostly when our pursued vision is clearly different from others around us. Treading new parts would always attract uncommon challenges aiming at keeping us backwards. Moving forward by embracing and learning such challenges rather than allowing it to break us is the best choice with the best solution to keep going places. By and large, we need to learn to start from where we are and with what we have. We should avoid waiting for the perfect moments or changes to occur in the current paradigm. The truth is, if we aren't moving forward, we are moving backwards and moving forward is a choice which can't be imposed on anyone. It's up to an individual to identify the need to move forward in the right direction regardless of obstacles we come across. In desiring new levels in life, we might get stuck in a rut from time to time, which is a common phenomenon, but it's up to us whether or not to get ourselves screwed in any situation we find ourselves in. A strong desire to be progressive would enable us to act and rise above circumstances trying to limit us in life. Alan Lakein, the American author said, "Planning is bringing the future into the present so that you can do something about it now".

I would like to share the story of the football manager who was hired by a local football club which played in the conference league. The new manager was hired after the previous manager was sacked by another football club in a higher division with just two weeks left to start the league. Due to the introduction of a new kind of dynamics and philosophy, also the pressure the team experienced four ridiculous defeats in a consecutive manner. Going from frying pan to fire, both the board of directors, club fans and the press began to raise serious concerns of the new manager's ability to get their desire that season, which was getting promoted to the next league above them. Due to the fear of relegation and losing sponsorships, an emergency meeting was held to decide the future of the manager with the club. After hours of controversial motions, the manager was allowed to express his understanding of the situation in simple terms. I would like to appreciate the club as a whole for giving me the opportunity to be its manager. I could see the situation clearer than ever in which I take full responsibility for. Mind all, if l fail the club, my coaching career remains in the blink and my credibility and suitability for the future would be in serious doubt, so am here to deliver and nothing more. Also, I quite understand the various motions on ground which includes if I should go or remain. I remember and still stick to my promise and never ready to compromise for any reason in which I strongly believe the best thing to be done is to keep moving and remain more hopeful than ever. Of course, speeding is good but moving forward is what manners are. I see tough times as a misleading indicator and we can only win if we refuse to be defeated and the fastest is not always the best. And here he came to the end of his speech. To cut the long story short, the new manager later made some adjustments within the team and kept moving forward by winning most matches and drew its best with stronger teams within the league. The team ended up with the second position on the league table falling three points behind the cup winners. The fact to be ironed out is, the new manager was busy studying the current situation on ground before making reasonable changes which enabled him to move towards the club's desire. One main insight which l personally draw from the club's story is, an arrow can only be shot by pulling it backward. So when life is dragging us back with difficulties, it means that it's going to launch us into something great. So all we need to do is to just keep our focus and keep aiming for peak results through effective performances. Another point is that we sometimes have to go through the worst to get the best. As we all know, life remains a journey and never a final destination, we are bound to record both failures and successes at various points but most important thing is the ability to keep moving.

    My message at this point is simple, loving others is good but the best is to avoid waiting for those who are not ready and willing to move because it amounts to a waste of time and ends with regrets. That's why it's paramount to move once it's the right time to do so because you can never please or understand all parties around you. Life is very complicated when you have standards, people call it attitude, when you are simple people try to cheat you and when you try to cheat them, they call you smart. Having a progressive mind set would always avoid us from being stagnant, it's better to be slow and sure as a result of learning rather than being locked up by circumstances or imaginary situations. According to Dana Arcuri, in her book: reinventing you, *"Similar to a butterfly, I've gone through a metamorphosis, been released from my dark cocoon, embraced my wings, and soared"*. Reinvesting ourselves is what makes us different kinds of person in any endeavour and that's why we need to keep updating ourselves with relevant knowledge and skills.

Above all, just as Conrad Hilton said, "success seems to be connected with action. Successful people keep moving, they make mistakes, but they don't quit and this is what brings out the best in them". Many do talk of making next moves at the right time while leaving the required job undone, I do see this as technical procrastination due to the fear of unknown risk. Just as Abraham Maslow, the American psychologist once said, "You will either step forward into growth or you will step back into safety". According to Andy Frisella, "Instead of thinking how hard your journey is, think how great your story will be". Just as Sylvester Stallone said in the movie Rocky Balboa, The world ain't all sunshine and rainbows. It is a very mean and nasty place and it will beat you to your knees and keep you there permanently if you let it. You, me, or nobody is going to hit as hard as life. But it ain't how hard you hit; it's about how hard you can get hit, and keep moving forward. One essential thing about being progressive in life is having the ability to set right and attainable goals. Zig Ziglar, the American author and motivational speaker said, "A goal properly set is halfway reached. No more no less". And my simple advice is, Don't watch the clock; do what it does. Keep going, according to Sam Levenson. To keep moving is to keep growing and once growth is given a consistent priority fulfilment is always the end product.

Three Vital Nuggets

"The greatest way to live with honour in this world is to be what we pretend to be. All above, never feel ashamed for prioritizing yourself. Remember, you've got to take care of yourself before you can start taking care of others".
Socrates

Having quenched my thirst on the need to write a book on choice in terms of its definition, importance and how it has helped the best discover and distinguish themselves from the rest. I would like to discuss three powerful insights which I tagged the vital nuggets coined from the story of Jacob in the bible when he was in the house of Laban which are: playing your game, running your race and living your life. Jacob was blessed in the long run because he asked Laban the right question at the right time, which was.......... "when shall I provide for my own house also"? (Gen 30 vs 30), the powerful question was the main turning point which facilitated taking the right steps and facing huge challenges before he located his blessing at Bethel mightily (Gen 35 vs 12). The question was a matter of 'should I go or should I stay', no matter the choice he had made, he would have ended up somewhere. But bear in mind, if he had not gone to provide for his own house, he wouldn't have been a distinguished figure in the bible history today. In reality, having the ability to step out of your comfort zone is the best way to avoid being a liability to yourself and others around you. One thing I have learned from wrestlers while in the ring is that there's nothing like friendship, mercy or forgiveness, you just have to do whatever is required of you to win or else no one would be interested in investing in you.

PLAY YOUR GAME

Believe it or not, there is no one else who is just like you. In terms of your physical appearance, your voice, personal traits, habits, intelligence, personal taste and sorts, this makes you one of a kind in the whole universe. Even your fingerprints distinguish you from every other human being in times past, present or future. As a matter of fact, there's no point burying your ambition for the sake of pleasing others. However, most do so by neglecting the reality of doing what they were supposed to do at the right time due to the fear of the unknown or pleasing others. Jacob's decision was a typical reflection of diligence and intelligence. By diligence, that is, knowing and understanding what he wanted and its cost in life before going for it and by intelligence, foreseeing the future of his departure or staying back before making a choice. Another personality of note in the Bible was King Solomon who knew what it would cost him to build the temple before starting to avoid confusion.

Jacob made up his mind to stand for himself and his household which is also a reflection of liberation, in fact, humanity without liberation is meaningless and that is why the battle for liberation continues from one generation to another. Without Jacob liberating himself, hardly would he have been able to attain significance in his lifetime. Above all, no matter your age, status or circumstances, never allow anything i.e. system or culture in place, belief or past experiences of yours or others disallow you from achieving your goal.

Playing our game is a matter of taking those vital steps towards achieving our desirable life and not walking or running simply because others want us to only place and fix where they want us to be. We are better off playing our game and making mistakes which facilitates more experience and growth rather than sitting on the fence amounting us to nothing. Referring to one remarkable quote of the evergreen musical legend Bob Marley: Beginnings are usually scary, and endings are usually sad, but it's everything in between that makes it all worth living. Meaning, taking transforming steps could be packed with the fear of the unknown or disastrous imagination but taking bold steps like Jacob is what creates a difference and real meaning to one's life. Bear in mind, endings are usually sad, every man is bound to give up the ghost at some point but whatever he does is remembered of him

Playing your game, place you in full control of your life just as William Ernest Henley wrote in his poem 'I am the master of my fate: I am the captain of my soul'. The truth is that when you are inspired by your goals, you believe and act on them, then you will accomplish them. No one would have known Barack Obama as the 44th U.S. President, if he hadn't played his game well and with focus, even when the supposed closest mate discouraged his step and practically left him to his fate without support and made him realize he cannot amount to what he is aspiring to be, he did not relent but rather pressed further in achieving his goal and making her see the success of his vision on the long run. At the end Obama was celebrated and honored because he played his game with focus and the utmost realization that he is the carrier of the vision and not his wife. In totality, having the ability to play your game is the best way you disallow others from influencing or determining what you could become or attain in life i.e. avoiding being limited by others or position our destiny at their wish and they impose it on us. The gospel truth is that, to feel good about yourself, design the type of life you truly want to live. You're in control, so get excited about the opportunity to enhance your growth. The fact is, no one owes you the responsibility of understanding and supporting your vision, it is up to you to get up and play your game before winning. Above all, bear it in mind that life is a game, play it; Life is a challenge, meet it;

THREE VITAL NUGGETS

Life is an opportunity, Capture it. I do tell young people to be determined to do the hard work to actualize their dreams as the future would always give account of how the past was spent. And that's why one needs to be bold enough to discover himself in terms of who he is meant to become in his lifetime and not build for another man all his life. Playing one's game also includes knowing when to make the next move or attain the next level having overcome certain challenges or achieve specific goals. The point is, staying too long on the same level amounts to stagnancy and failure on the long-run. We need to improve ourselves by seeking better opportunities and exploring new avenues because every little step we make creates a huge long-run difference and bears repeating the same thing and expecting new outcomes amounts to insanity.

RUN YOUR OWN RACE

As a strong believer of philosophy which contains elements of spirituality. I have come to realize that those who wait for things to change before making moves never get informed by things when about to change. It's better to get up at the right time, face down standing challenges and not dodging or making nice excuses as in why not to do whatever needs to be done to build and live a desirable life rather than expecting magic or wishing someone comes your way to get things done for you. Bearing in mind that the day of accountability would eventually catch up with everyone at some point in life and every man would be known for whatever he lived for. According to James Brian Hellwig, The Ultimate Warrior, "Every man's heart one day beats its final beat, his lungs breathe their final breath and if what that man did in his life makes the blood pulse through the body of others and makes them believe deeper in something larger than life, then his essence, his spirit will be immortalised". By and large, running your own race is a matter of focusing on what you are trying to build and achieve without allowing the progress of others to distract you and never compete or compare with anyone. No matter how wide deceit might spread and lies keep flying, the truth would always prevail and be established at the end of it all. In life, either one faces whatever is being faced with in reality or such gets ruined and faced down by the same situation.

Coming to the philosophical interpretation of the dream Jacob had at Bethel regarding the battle with the angel in (Genesis 28) the fact is that anyone desiring success would need to do the needful and not just be procrastinating or wait for what he deserves which could be robbed off him unlike the case of Esau. Struggling with the angel is a sign of him knowing and understanding his goal in life which is to be blessed and missing the angel's blessing might cost him fulfilling his destiny. Extracting more understanding from Jacob's story, he cherished his goal of being fulfilled in life from his uncle's house and never lost focus regardless of the number of years he spent in his house. Jim Rohn, once said, "Goals, there's no telling what you can do when you get inspired by them. There's no telling what you can do when you believe in them. And there's no telling what will happen when you act upon them". The truth above all, when your goals inspire you, when you believe and act on them, you will accomplish them no matter the obstacles, cost, challenges and setbacks. However, believing in what you could become in life is essential before making moves mostly when others doubt your vision or dream. Michele Ruiz once said, "If people are doubting how far you can go, go so far that you can't hear them anymore".

LIVE YOUR LIFE

According to the English writer, Lewis Carroll, "In the end, we only regret the chances we didn't take". Having been a life coach and a writer for years, I have come to realize the fact that, apart from ignorance, fear has held many back from living up to their potential. The Brazilian lyricist, Paulo Coelho, did make it clear that, "There is only one thing that makes a dream impossible to achieve: the fear of failure". According to Dr Prem Jagyasi, "The most common regret that people have on their deathbed is that they lived their life according to the desires of others, not how they wanted to". The third lesson I learnt from Jacob was that after making the best decision for his life i.e. playing his game, taking the rightful steps i.e. running his own race, he lived a fulfilled life. (Gen 35 vs 12). We are the best of ourselves when we accept to live a life without limitation. According to Les Brown, "Life has no limitations, except the ones you make". By and large, the impact we make in life is based on the choices we make whether we live it or we ditch it. To live our best, we need to go for passion and be happy with ourselves, learn to live in the present by taking lessons from the past and preparing for tomorrow, and spend our time wisely as it waits for no one.

I would like to share the story of a young man whose education was supported by his parents. He was made to study architecture as his father was a well-known personality within the construction industry. The young man was sound academically and he made good grades at the end of his study. But what changed the paradigm was while attending various self-discovery seminars and workshops during his final year at the University, he discovered being an architect wasn't the best for him. He discovered more of himself and his potential through the swot analysis table. In terms of his strength, he could communicate effectively and tirelessly and love to initiate solutions to philosophical challenges people do face in their lives. He has the ability to think and reason critically, effective listening techniques and possesses a high sense of confidence in whatever he does. According to Tony Robbins, "Self-awareness is one of the rarest of human commodities". I don't mean self-consciousness where you're limiting and evaluating yourself. I mean being aware of your own patterns. There's no point in playing yourself down just to please people. As the story continues, upon discovering himself he began to design his future which was absolutely different from what his father wanted him to be. In one of the workshops which he attended, he discovered he's responsible for whatever he becomes in life and he has to make his own choice and not anyone doing that for him. Aside from studying and creating time to read more books on philosophy, personal development and also listen to a lot of motivational tapes from various authorities in the world of business and other relevant fields. In the long run, he began to invest in himself. According to Robin Sharma, "Investing in yourself is the best investment you can make. It will not only improve your life; it will improve the lives of all those around you". Upon graduating from the university, he appreciated his parents and made it clear that he preferred becoming a life coach and not an architect, which is as good as living his dad's second dream and not his. He stressed that he understood the importance of education which includes empowering and enlightening the mind and facilities ideas. However, he could have his life more meaningful and attain heights while helping people design their lives and grow rather than designing buildings and structures. Note, upon discovering himself, he never saw studying architecture as a mistake or a waste of time but rather as a stepping stone towards his calling. He understood education had enlightened and empowered him. According to J.K. Rowling, "Understanding is the first step to acceptance, and only with acceptance can there be recovery".

In a nutshell, no matter the number of years one might have wasted through ignorance, it's better to start late than not start at all. Nothing stops a late bloomer from excelling in life other than themselves. Colonel Sanders, the founder of the fast food company, KFC never started the business until the age of sixty-six. Jamie Vardy, the English football star never started his career until the age of 61 making him a late bloomer. Relating the young man's story to that of Jacob. He never saw his life with a dead end simply because he spent over 20 years serving his uncle. He knew there's more of what he could achieve in life rather than staying back. According to Tony Robbins, "The past does not equal the future unless you live there". Back to the young man, He began to network with other speakers and life coaches and also took courses to understand more of what he needs to know such as designing and achieving goals both in business and in life. At some point, he took steps in setting up his business and getting deals in which his parents supported his commitment. Bear in mind, no reasonable being is ever ready to invest into someone without a direction or wasting his time. My next point is, success is not magic. Paul Meyer once said, "Productivity is never an accident. It's the result of a commitment to excellence, intelligent planning and focused effort". While sharing his experience in becoming a successful coach, he did say and I strongly believe, "success in theory is a matter of adding one plus one to get two i.e. verbally simple but in reality, it's a matter of facing problems, various challenges and obstacles before attaining the peak". One glad thing about the young man was this, he never forced himself into or went to struggle unnecessarily within the construction industry and end up regretting. I'm glad the young man never felt intimidated in expressing himself to his family after graduation because a closed mouth is a ruined destiny and the untold truth is that there's no point playing low on yourself just to please people. Reality on ground, the young man would have ended up being his own destiny destroyer if not for the right choice he made at the end of his study.

Take This Home

"Even if you take the safe route through life, you might fail. If you follow your dreams, you might fail, too. But you might achieve them and that's what makes the difference".
Jim Carrey

According to Plato, no one is most hated than he that speaks the truth. Life is whatever we coin out of it. I do stamp it repeatedly that where we stand determines who sees us and who sees us determines what we get and how far we go. Life is not all about what others think, say or assume about us, rather what we chose to become is what makes us who we are. And whatever we chose to become in life eventually amounts to our destiny. Living with Regrets is avoidable but it's a choice that needs to be made. Our choice facilitates our decisions and actions which metamorphose into what we get in life. Either to work hard and create what we want, where we want to be and why we want to be there or we leave our lifetime for chances and circumstances to decide for us, it's up to us to make a choice. Apart from explaining how one could be made or broken through choice making, this book has pointed out the power of one's choice and the need to make good choices in life. Making no choice or perpetrating what to be and where to be in life is never an option towards living a successful life but only facilities ending up with regrets. Having the ability to drive your world that is, having full control and taking full responsibility of our lives, setting a higher and reasonable standard for ourselves backed with a peak performance are choices that would enable us go the extra mile in life rather than dwelling within philosophical vacuums and intellectual bondages or vacuum created by unknown parameters. Being the real version of ourselves and our choice to be enlightened equips us ahead of challenges and opportunities with the aim of making better choices to take further steps in life rather than being stagnant at an unexpected point in life. Fears, threats and obstacles are part of life and these are battles to be faced and fought to determine our suitability for a fulfilled life. By the way, not every dream gets fulfilled and not every vision gets actualized. We choose to either make our dream a reality by fighting for it with all we've got or make it a mere slogan by ditching it and later following the crowd. Of course, fears, threats or any form of obstacles are inevitable factors of life and are determining factors to separate the best from the better, the strongest from the stronger ones. That's why we need to be bold and face our fears, and also give what it takes to overcome anything holding us backward. A driver aiming to move his car forward wouldn't place the gear in reverse while the gear is in his control and later place the blame on circumstances or previous mistakes. We've gotten dark sides at one point or the other in our lives but the best way to handle it to let the past go is by placing it behind us and aiming for a better tomorrow. And to live our possible best tomorrow we need to start by living it in the present. By implication, we should begin to understand and follow the reality of the moment. Regardless of the numerous failures and successes we record in life, we should never stop trying and taking on other challenges to keep us from moving forward and better than our previous state. There is a lot to gain from life once right choices could be made and we could do away with negative voices to act but just focus on our conviction. For a better reflection of how impactful choice making is in all aspects of life. I would like to share the story of a lady who happened to be one of the facilitators at a youth seminar where I happened to be a guest speaker. I could remember vividly; I spoke on the 7 Laws of Productivity:

a book which I authored some years ago. It all happened a few years ago, while she was a member of a youth movement which was formed with the aim of fighting for youth rights such as employment, educational support and other institutional benefits. The town where she lived had gotten the wide gap between the rich and the less privileged than ever. After staging numerous protests and campaigns against the government for neglecting the future generation, they eventually caught the attention of the international community at large. It was speculated that only the children of the elite are considered for white collar jobs and non-indigenes are hired for the blue collar jobs within the town where the speaker grew up. The government of the day was pressured to act but did little more than expected. To the surprise of all, the youth president called a press conference without the consent of other executive members of the movement to appreciate the government for providing employment for over 65 percent of the movement and promised never to protest or do media campaigns as their expectations had been met. Can this be the energetic president who was believed to be a no nonsense person? Upon investigation, it was found out that less than three percent of the movement were employed by the government on a short-term contract. This led to a serious controversy with the movement and the president was called to give answers to the many questions desired by its members and the media. Further reports were made regarding the sudden transformed lifestyle of the president without a traceable source as he was a well-known primary school teacher. Few months later, two government officials were arrested for misappropriation of funds which was brought to public knowledge. After further interrogations, it was revealed that the president of the movement was a regular night visitor at the state house who got paid for briefing government officials and politicians on issues discussed at meetings and steps about to be taken. He was reported to have supplied personal details of members who stood to be a potential threat to the government which led to a lot of unjustifiable arrests of the movement members and detained without trial. Another controversial question was; can this be the man we trusted this much? To worsen matters, bank statements were later published on various dallies, followed by a clip from a surveillance camera footage in one of the government buildings and so the cat was let out of the bag. This led to a serious political propaganda used by the opposition party against the party in government and they began to lose their popularity. As this situation has created a winning edge for the strongest opposition party, they devised a strategy by merging with other political parties and went further and converse with the youth movement and adopted their new president in person of the former vice president as the running mate of the gubernatorial candidate. In addition, members of the movement were also promised some key positions within the cabinet and massive employment. In a few words, the opposition party won the election and the former youth president could no longer have a place to hide himself because his god fathers had considered him unfit for their purpose and he brought huge shame to his family due to his mistrust behaviour. He was a product of his choice and that's why no matter where we find ourselves in life either by merit or by chance, trust should be our foundation and brand. In the course of writing this book, I did remember a short drama aired on television many years ago. It was all about a young lady who was wooed by two young men Eton and George, both rich but one short and bald-headed. After a long period of contemplating, she decided to consult a soothsayer, from her point of view, it was crystal clear she admired Eton more than George because Eton seems to be cool. After reading her palm, the soothsayer revealed that if she marries Eton, there would be a speedy progress for 10years and stagnation would take over which might lead to a separation. In the case of George, there would be slow progress but persistent however, the relationship would last and be joyful. She then asked if it's possible to have the situation swapped. The soothsayer laughed and asked her, who changes the direction of the wind? No one, she replied. The lady left in a worrisome mood. After explaining the situation to her aunty, she was advised to choose one and leave the other as far as you know what you want in life. You can't eat your cake and have it, however, your choice becomes your destiny. As a matter of fact, she ended up marrying George. In life, choices are too nice and paramount to be ignored and not making a choice at all in controversial and challenging situations makes us worse off and place us in a more regrettable state because we would have been better off trying and failing. We can choose to be the solution to our problems or the problem to our solution and no one can seek blessing from the one who is yet to bless himself. Our ability to make right choices makes us master of our own unique destiny by following the core values explained in this book. From experience, I realized that the platform for self-discovery lies in the ability of choosing those we associate ourselves with, the right people help you grow towards becoming emotionally and intellectually independent and vice versa. Truth be told, nothing else transforms one other than choosing to take the right direction in a consistent manner and not remaining stationed like a tree. This is the way we can be progressive in life because it involves planning before acting in various aspects of our life such as finance and professional career and social engagements. In a free world, we might also choose to do nothing by pretending rather than taking action. However, it's up to us to choose to design our own life the way we want it to be or as it has been done by someone else. As Shakespeare uniquely observed, "The fault is not in the stars, but in ourselves". We created our current circumstances by our past choices. We have both the ability and the responsibility to make better choices beginning from today. As this book is titled, GET IT RIGHT, YOUR CHOICE IS YOURDESTINY: I'm sure it might still be hard for many to believe because taking responsibility for a desirable future is a tough choice in which only the few are ready to make. Ralph Waldo Emerson, the American philosopher, once said," the only person you are destined to become is the person you decide to be". This is simply the truth because we are products of our personal choice and our lives depend so much on the choices we make. To back up my point of view, the principle of sowing and reaping remains inevitable and that is why as human beings we sow whatever we want to reap later on. The story of the youth movement president is a better illustration of the same principle. He would have wished, never to have been caught in between but for every action, there is an equal and opposite reaction. The president was yet to understand that whatever goes upward would always return to its original state and that is why we need to think deeply before making our choices because our choices are typical reflections of who we are and lands us wherever we found ourselves in life. In life, to achieve your goals, live your dreams and actualize your long-term visions to have a sense of fulfilment, you need to do what you have to do until you can do what you want to do. According to Oprah Winfrey who said and I quote, "We need to make choices to live our life before it leaves us, to reach our goal before it kicks us out once our time is up". She also said her philosophy is that not only are you responsible for your life, but doing the best at this moment puts you in the best place for the next moment, that is, being unwavering in your thoughts and actions {advancement}. Doing something different creates something different, it's a choice to be successful and it's a choice to go for something big. By and large, your choice is your destiny, even when you make wrong decisions as far as you are in charge of your life, it's up to you to either change it or abide by it. If you don't take the responsibility of changing the paradigm of your unpleasant life, no one would change it for you. The zeal to change for the best is what graduates us from being unstoppable by mastering self-confidence and being the master of our life. According to a friend of mine, Philippa Gittens, "take ownership of your life and what direction it goes in, this is the most powerful choice we could make in life". And just as Drake Graham did mention, "It's never too late to realize what you want in your life and it's never wrong to fight for it". And also bear in mind that not everyone will understand your journey, the route, distance, gains, loss, wins, failures, achievement etc. The best choice anyone could make is to focus on his own path, holding the fort strongly without wavering while allowing others to focus on theirs, this is because the picture in your mind of whom you are trying and striving to be is unique to you alone. Life is about choices. Some we regret, some we're proud of. Some will haunt us forever. My message is simple, "We are whatever we chose to be", according to Graham Brown. Once again, Jacob was convinced what he could become in his mind before pursuing it in real sense, philosophically our mind is like a parachute and all we have to do is open it to make it function and to transform our lives.

www.ingramcontent.com/pod-product-compliance
Lightning Source LLC
Chambersburg PA
CBHW050436010526
44118CB00013B/1554